Pathway Through Memories

People Who Lived in Burloak Waterfront Park

David Woodward

I hope you enjoy learning about Carol's entire life.

Best Wishes

David Woodward

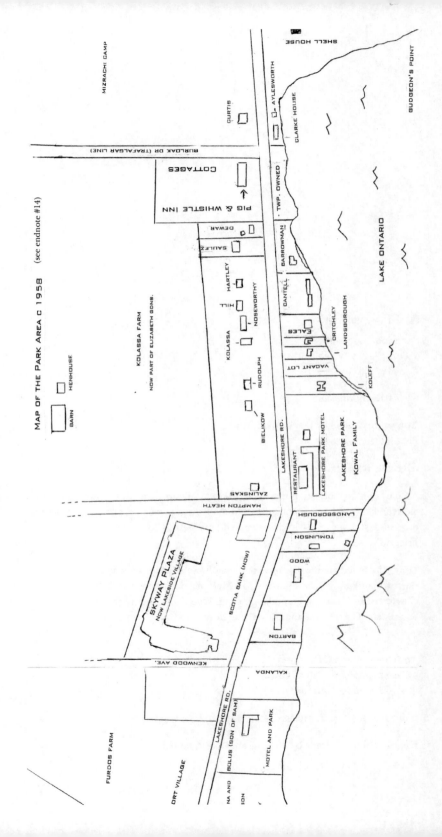

MAP OF THE PARK AREA c 1958   (see endnote #14)

 FriesenPress

Suite 300 - 990 Fort St
Victoria, BC, V8V 3K2
Canada

www.friesenpress.com

Photos included are mostly those of the author except for the chapters on the Barrowman family (Carol Barrowman McKane, daughter), the Koleff family chapter, (Carol Bristow, granddaughter, and the Kowal family chapter, Jeanette Spasuk and Carrie Pentland, Kowal daughters.

ISBN
978-1-5255-2063-1 (Hardcover)
978-1-5255-2064-8 (Paperback)
978-1-5255-2065-5 (eBook)

1. BIOGRAPHY & AUTOBIOGRAPHY, PERSONAL MEMOIRS

Distributed to the trade by The Ingram Book Company

TABLE OF CONTENTS

TO THE READER

Other than the majestic view, the most noticeable feature of Burloak Waterfront Park is the paved trail winding like a stream throughout its entire length. Extending from east to west over 2000 feet, the trail is smooth and measures a good four metres wide. Punctuated along the edge, twenty-seven benches are planned to be installed by mid 2018. To the casual visitor walking the path they will be conscious of the lake view, the beaches that have access, the foliage, natural plants and animals, as well as passing walkers like themselves. But to me this is a pathway through memories. As I meander along enjoying the view, I notice what everyone else sees but mostly I remember the people who lived in the place where I am standing. Ten families lived throughout the park area during the past seventy-five years, though none of them lived there that long. Who were these people in this small community between Bronte, one and a half miles to the east, and Burlington, five miles to the west? What was it like living in the forties and fifties into the eighties and beyond on the shore of magnificent Lake Ontario?

My objective is to describe some of the residents who were very interesting people from diversified backgrounds, education, and livelihoods. Almost everyone was an immigrant who came here looking to improve his or her life. People on both sides of the road will be described as to where they lived and some interesting details of their lives. They were rich and poor, talented and ordinary. Indeed some could even be described as eccentric. As far as daily life is concerned, I hope to tell how they lived and whiled away the hours when life was less frenetic. Neighbours were more private in those years than they are today and often one didn't know much about the people next door. Nevertheless, people knew something of each other for quite a distance. They often stopped to chat when passing by. Local gossip always filled in blanks. We visited other homes or farms in this small area and gradually got to know the area as our community. The need for certain daily requirements led one to see if one's neighbour could assist in providing it. Such things as a meal at the restaurant, water to drink, or who to call to put in a septic tank, for example.

Burloak Waterfront Park is relatively new since many parcels where houses once stood languished undeveloped for the past twenty years waiting for residents to sell the final bits to the City of Burlington and/or the Region of Halton. Part of this property was a park since the thirties — the first five hundred feet from the west side. That part is where the children's playground is situated today and ranging to the west boundary opposite Hampton Heath Road and south to the lake from the Lakeshore Highway, old King's Highway number 2. Starting in 1940, immigrant settlers started to buy lots commencing at the Trafalgar Road end, now Burloak Drive. My immigrant grandparents chose a piece for their retirement home right in the middle and hence my connection to a local history that must be told before it is all forgotten.

You will not find this community listed in any official "communities" found in various local history books. Mail was delivered there with the address "RR #2 Freeman", which was the closest post office in the early fifties. Freeman was located about five miles west at Brant Street and Plains Road. There was no school or local church focus but there was a pub, The Pig and Whistle Inn, at the corner of what is now Burloak and Lakeshore intersection. The Inn also included a number of rental cottages. Across from what is now Hampton Heath and Lakeshore corner was a restaurant with cabins; later a motel and a restaurant with seven acres of parkland. Even a trailer camp rested there for a few years. Several farms resided along the north side of road also, the largest being 86 acres.

I am also writing this book for my grandchildren and local people for when they get to that point in their lives that they want to know what came before. I hope to show how people took a chance and a risked leaving behind the comfort of family and friends for a better life in a new land. I love walking the path through memories of them. Just like the immigrants

DAVID WOODWARD

of today they added a richness of culture and experience to the Canadian landscape that changed Canada for the better. These people were in many ways ordinary but they achieved success in their lives and have left an enduring legacy to the landscape. Their stories are unique and anything but ordinary.

DEDICATION

This book I dedicate first to my loving wife, Ann-Louise, who has encouraged me in the project. We have been married 50 years as of the year of publication and she has put up with the many hours of discussion of the contents over the years. On the computer night after night over long stretches of time and then ignoring the project for a while has demanded many hours of dedication by me. But it takes a toll over the significant others who can only watch and bide their time. Not once did Ann-Louise ever complain to me about that. I owe her gratitude for her ideas on making the project more appealing to the reader.

The other folks who deserve to share the dedication are the characters described in print throughout the book. I honour their memory as most have passed on but some family members and descendants still remain in the area.

Three individuals I owe a special dedication to are the following:

From my grandfather, I was able to have a gentle, kind, and loving guide in every facet of my life. He and my family let me have freedom to explore and follow my dreams without judgment. I always had a safe environment and a refuge from whatever hurly-burly goes on in a young boy's life. My granddad taught me so many skills in everyday life from woodworking to the love of history. Patience and courage was his motto and he gave me the strength to persevere through many of life's challenges as the years went on.

From Bert Jordan I gained so much knowledge about gardening and awareness of the world. Our discussion on long walks and nights sipping coffee over stories of his past opened doors for me that never would have been possible without him.

Indeed, my third career after 32 years of teaching and being a principal in Halton is now gardening. Bert was a landscape gardener who worked on two local estates. I have worked for fifteen years now enjoying this occupation. His example was the inspiration.

James Barrowman was concurrently mentor with the previous two. He listened intently to most of my ideas and always questioned me as to why I thought a certain way. We discussed current events, religion, ethics, morals, philosophy, art, music and literature. When I arrived out for the weekends and holidays, I couldn't wait to visit him and his family. To him I owe the ability to reflect on my own behaviour and my motives for doing things. Most of all I love what he taught me to appreciate in the world of the arts.

ACKNOWLEDGEMENTS

How to thank those that have made it possible to fulfill a dream is always difficult. Nevertheless, no book is possible without those who provide information, stimulation, encouragement, and ideas to the author. As I have already said, my wife and family have given me undying encouragement and listened to me talk about the project without complaint. That includes my children, Adam and Ashley, and grandchildren, Jackson, Will, Avery, and Emma. I also include my son-in-law, Rob MacGuire and my daughter-in-law, Callie. Thank you all for your great listening skills and support.

My travel friends Penny and Wally Coghlan and Diane and Stephen McCarthy who have put up with my chatter about the characters in my book for years without complaint when we toured European countries together.

To Adeline and Steve Rakowski, Carrie Pentland, and Jeanett Spasuk, thank you for pictures and stories of the past to keep the facts straight and in giving family background history on the Kowal family. They have been long time friends of my family.

I wish to particularly thank the late Ollie Bristow and her daughter, Carol, for pictures and stories of their family. They have become wonderful friends over the years through my interactions with four generations of the Koleff family. Carol also assisted in editing her family's chapter.

Margaret Landsborough, 96 years of age, I thank wholeheartedly for her friendship and encouragement with the story of her family.

My neighbour, Ruth Adams, for helping proofread some chapters. She is great listener and keen observer of detail.

Shirley Bottaro for her help about her father, Constable

Harvey Hunt I also wish to acknowledge here.

Carol Barrowman has been an undying source of information and understanding as I tried to describe her family and struggles over the years. Pictures from her have helped tell her story I hope.

The publishing team at FriesenPress whose ongoing assistance in improving all aspects of the book for final publication have been superlative in every respect. I list those who went out of their way to encourage and prod me to improvement as: Code Workun, Samantha Paulus, and especially, Miko Heddle.

A view of today's park from the west looking
east showing beaches and a little bay.

Preface:
Lake Ontario

Lake Ontario, farthest right, is the smallest but
a deep lake which rarely freezes over

Situated in almost the heart of the continent, five great lakes were formed about 14,000 years ago as the mile or two high glaciers gouged out basins to hold the meltwater of their former selves. The smallest, but one of the deepest of these is Lake Ontario on the north shore of which this story takes place. Our lake is a beautiful lake. Most of the time it is calm and serene, the picture of peace and tranquility. At other times, this great body of water roars with the anger of crashing waves and bitter winds. The roughness of these occasions sees the water colour turn to muddy brown along the shale shores that are reduced to soil and clay in a short time. Indeed, our small stretch of shoreline saw 75 feet of land lost to the ever encroaching lake within 45 years. In the early days of exploration and settlement, numerous ships sank in a matter of minutes by the onset of gales. A great example this can be found in the two ships sunk by a gale during the War of 1812. They rest 300 feet down on the bottom near the opposite shore of the Niagara peninsula off Port Dalhousie. This site lies directly opposite Burloak Waterfront Park.

In three of the seasons, reflected light paints a rainbow of beautiful colours on the surface of the water just as a painter wields his brush. Far to the horizon and within a thousand feet from the shore the lake is a deep blue in summer. Closer to shore, it blends into lighter blue and sometimes a turquoise where ripple waves lap against the shore. In spring and autumn, this can give a cold or morose look depending on the sun. Then the grey days turn the water to a whiteness that makes the water almost invisible to the eye. Some winter days host a deep blue body of water across the whole lake surface. Raging storms can occur in a few minutes out of nowhere from what appears the other side of the lake, producing white caps that look like horses spewing their foam in full, furious gallop. The storms can come from the east and west but the most violent, seem to come from the east. Waves build up over the surface of the three hundred mile length.

There are many moods on Lake Ontario which transform themselves to the human condition and make those who bear witness, either melancholy or euphoric as they arise to meet the day. A window on the lake is like a moving picture that draws the viewer in. It is always changing. On the surface, humanity also creates the changes that transform the scene, from gigantic lake ships plying the waters to deliver or transport their contents. Small sailboats in a regatta, launches that throb from diesel engines, and a barge or water skier are common everyday sights. The resident lake dwellers watch with fascination while others are oblivious. For me, I was always fascinated, and kept binoculars on the window sill for closer observation.

When I started teaching, I lived at my grandparents' home on the lake in what is now Burloak Park for the first year. After a tiring day at school, attempting to unlock the minds and creativity of my junior school pupils, it was so relaxing to come home and sit by the edge of the shore. In early September

DAVID WOODWARD

staring at the beauty this wondrous lake on which I grew up as a child, gave me renewed energy. Sitting in contemplation of the environment there recharged my will to carry on and plan for another day.

If you haven't lived by a lake or large body of water perhaps you haven't noticed the power of the water to influence your daily life. It is not just what you see but what you hear from the wind to the cry of the birds and sound of fog horns or boats chugging by. Then there are the smells like seaweed, which, in our lake's case, is really algae. The smell of stinky fish washed ashore sometimes makes you gag. In the fifties, these were usually alewife fish we called, "shiners" because of their silvery skin. This usually happened in later summer.

But the winds blowing off the surface of our great lake sometimes blew sweet fragrances of freshness or damp cold. They even carried the flower pollen swirling from nearby fields and gardens. When I was a teenager I remember one night I couldn't sleep but had to stare out a the brightly-lit moonlight that danced in a path across the water. The window was open and somewhere nearby was the sweet smell of strawberries finding its way into my bedroom window. Those moments were intoxicating and have stayed with me all these years.

Speaking of moonlight nights, who could not fail to stare at the horizon as a great golden orange-yellow ball rose from the edge the horizon? Its race to get to the other side of the sky by morning was its quest. In my youth, these sightings, particularly in late August and September, pulled at my heart-strings and I yearned for a particular girl I wished could be there too. Where do these emotions come from and how do they arise just from a sight of the moon over the water with its shimmering path? Who knows? But such is the lure of a moon over water. It is free and always available from season to season, year upon year. Here in east Burlington at the present Burloak Park or in Spencer Smith Park at the western end of town, I am sure viewers everywhere experience the same rush of feeling on these nights. I know I continue to be drawn there with my camera hoping to catch the right moment and relive it through photographs on my computer. Such is the life along the shore of this natural wonder we take for granted. Burloak Waterfront Park is a treasure that can be enjoyed by all for merely the cost of time.

For a child, exploring a seashore or lakeshore, is always an adventure in discovery and wonder. Our lake never disappointed. Along the very edge, walking barefoot, one could be amazed at the myriad coloured stones and glass. All were ground smooth and rounded from the action of the waves rubbing them against each other over time. Every visit led to a collection of a few or many wet shining stones. No one cared whether they were sedimentary, igneous, or metamorphic stones and rocks. The only thing that mattered was their lustrous beauty. When the wetness evaporated, the dull colours remained and the gatherer splashed colour back over them with the water. Most of all it was fun skipping these perfectly round stones across the lake surface. Each child tried to outdo the other with the number of skips and the distanced traveled when he cast the stone. Most fit perfectly between the forefinger and the thumb and if you held your hand at a particular angle parallel to the lake surface, your stone would do its magic. How many hours were spent skipping these stones? Today, the shingle stones have been replaced on the Burloak Park beaches by river rocks and they do not skip! The round river rocks, however, are better at breaking the power of the waves.

Sand swallows flitted back and forth across the water's surface as they skimmed up insects which were everywhere. Close by in the first three feet or so of the lake banks these quick-flying birds emerged and delighted us with peeps and shows of flight mastery. Crayfish under rocks were a good hunt for a morning or early evening when swimming was done for the day. Occasionally one could locate a lurking carp or shiners galore splashing near the surface. Butterflies came by and caterpillars crawled. Dried up corn cobs we hollowed out to to make a pretend pipe, inserting a twig in the end for a stem. Then we would drop a line in or use a rod and tackle to see if we could catch fish. But the big ones were out in the lake in deep water as evidenced by the fishing boats with flat tops off Bronte. When they hauled in their catch in the Bronte harbour outside the grocery store, large containers of galvanized steel held huge lake trout and whitefish and other species which I cannot recall. Some of these were sold at Bill Hill's Grocery on the main street across from the fishing nets and pier. It was always delight to live by such a great lake.

The land on which the park is situated is known as Concession 4 SDS Lot 1, Nelson Township in the County of Halton. The first grant of this property was to a Mr. Stafford after the 1806 purchase from the Mississauga indigenous who occupied it until then. In the 1858 Tremaine Map, Con BF, Part Lot 1 is shown as owned by "C. S." In the 1877 map of Nelson Township in the Historical Atlas of Halton County, this part of Lot 1 is shown as owned by C. E. Thompson, a farmer, who sold it in 1929 to Hughes Cleaver, a lawyer and developer.[1]

I have written an account that follows with the hope of preserving the memories of some remarkable people, citizens of Burlington and Nelson Township, before that. If I can impart what the fifties and sixties of the twentieth century were like in this part of the world, I will have succeeded. It is my hope that you enjoy the journey through and around the environs of Burloak Park. Maybe my memories can bring the reader a new enjoyment of their environment.

1

The Barrowman Family

James Barrowman oil paintings of Lois, Carol and Self Portrait of the artist

I believe the first family to settle on the land that is now Burloak Park were the Barrowmans — James, Lois, and their two daughters, Carol and Dalzelle. The Scottish name Dalzelle is pronounced "Dee-al". James, or Jim, as people called him was a dreamer. He was a true artist which he became for most of his later life until he died. James left Coatbridge, Scotland for emigration to Canada on the *SS* Cameronia in January 1932. He was 25 years old.

Born in Muirkirk, Ayrshire, Scotland in 1907, James Barrowman had a wanderlust and desire to experience the new British Dominion of Canada to seek his fortune. I do not know whether Hamilton was a deliberate destination or not but that's where James settled and found work, listing his occupation in Scotland as turner/roller. He stated on the passenger manifest that he was to pursue the job of an insurance agent in Canada. In any case he landed a job at P.B. Yates. This company was one of the largest manufacturers of planers and other woodworking machinery in the world and still exists today. One day he had an accident that caused machinery to pierce his arm and temporarily paralyzed it. As a result of this after recuperation and therapy, James took up drawing and oil painting as a hobby. He had been ordered by his doctor to do something to concentrate his mind so that the pain would be less severe. Fine art was to become his lifelong love and he was a master of technique in oils. Try other painting media, James did, but he was unconvinced that acrylics, for example, would stand the test of time.

A special note is in order concerning James. He was a formidable figure of a man with a memorable countenance that put fear into my son whenever I took him to the Barrowmans' for a visit. In his youth, James had a great shock of wavy black hair that turned to a whitish gray as he matured over his lifetime. He was a striking figure with brown eyes that could pierce you to the core. I think that is what made my son so uncomfortable. It felt like he had an ability to peer right into one's soul.

James reminded me of what the philosopher Socrates must have been like. He was always probing and drawing one out trying to get to the essence of an idea. Perhaps it can be said that James was the personification of the consummate teacher. He rarely glanced upon a subject superficially, always wanting to dig deep inside the mind of whomever was the other half of the conversation. It didn't matter who the spectators were or who the company was in attendance, if the topic of conversation got around to art, every angle of the discussion was aired and explored. The person on the other side of the conversation was urged to reflect deeply about what he was saying and to articulate more fully the feelings behind his words or perceptions. However, I always had the feeling that he was a great listener and valued my opinions, never imposing his own except through a question.

Artist-Philosopher James Barrowman

One of his new paintings would be presented to me and having seen it for the first time, I would be asked to give my opinion about what it represented— how it made me feel— or how the colours added to the enjoyment for the viewer. Barrowman was a dramatic story teller. The listener could never forget the Scottish lilt to his voice that trailed to a whisper with a faint musicality in the slight whistle made by his mouth. This was particularly evident when he was telling a Boy Scout tale by the fireside as he relived his youth. I could converse with him for hours by the side of the lake following a corn on the cob dinner or after a hearty breakfast of kippers, eggs, bacon, toast and jam. The discussion was always about values and the moral issues of the day. I was very drawn to wanting to be in his company having a strong interest in philosophy from the time

I was about ten years old. To me, he was my Socrates.

Lois, his wife, came from Hamilton and was of Loyalist stock. Her United Empire Loyalist ancestor on her mother's side was David Peet of Connecticut. As Lois Evelyn Eastwood, she married James while working as an office clerk. Her siblings consisted of four brothers and one sister. She was a bookkeeper and excellent pianist. In fact until the day she moved it to her daughter's home in Kingston just before she died, Lois had her concert grand piano in the living room of her tiny cottage on Lakeshore Road. In 1937, Lois and Jim were proud parents to twin girls as mentioned above. Carol had been born with a defective heart, a condition known as "a blue baby". She received one of the first successful operations for this defect from Dr. Mustard in Toronto when she a young teenager.

Mr. Barrowman was the first settler on the eastern edge of the Burloak Park area as it is today. That is where he bought the narrow piece of land bordering the shore of Lake Ontario. It was tapered going east to west from almost the Trafalgar Line, now called Burloak Drive. Today the land would be worth several million dollars. By the steep bank and before the water's edge, lay a sloping beach piled high with flat shingle rocks, not the round river rocks in place there today. These rocks were more comfortable on the feet and one could pick up the small ones and have a great stone skipping competition with friends. Every kid and even adults did it. We all became experts at skipping beach stones, counting the number of skips each time. This was the first of two significant flat stone beaches along the length of the park. Amid the stones and rocks that shifted with every storm on Lake Ontario, came precious "sea glass" of a myriad of broken bottles washed to smoothness by the churning waves. In the wet palm of a hand these pieces of bright blue, sea green, aquamarine, and beer bottle brown appeared as gems to the child exploring the water's edge. When the glass bits were dry they lost their lustre because they needed polishing, but wet, they glowed with a particular beauty. On the seacoast one can find these coloured bits of sea glass for sale as jewelry.

Soon Jim, as he was known, and his wife Lois started to build a small temporary home to live in while they dreamed of their final abode in this fantastic location. Out to the east in the water ahead lay a jutting point called by neighbours

DAVID WOODWARD

Gudgeon's Point after the owner of the large house located there. Between that point and the jutting portion to the west we lived in a slight bay which gave refuge to the ships of a British Commodore, James Yeo as he mended the masts after the Battle for Lake Ontario. This was officially called the "Burlington Races" one hundred and fifty years before.[2] There is more of this story in chapter 5.

Straight ahead in the southeast, across the lake, lay the outline of the escarpment on the opposing shore as it wound its way along the horizon from Hamilton to Niagara. Straight out from the beach where the escarpment ended is Niagara-on-the-Lake, though one cannot see it with the naked eye. On a clear day now one can see some mist occasionally from the falls in that direction and some misty towers of Niagara Falls, but that is a not too frequent sighting. James must have thought he arrived at paradise.

The Construction of the Barrowman House with a Slate Roof

Lois and Jim built their small home with fireplace and slate roof consisting of a bedroom, sitting room, kitchen and bathroom. They had a marble hearth and fireplace. This was to last until they were able to afford their future dwelling providing room for themselves and their twin daughters. A separate wooden two story garage was constructed to the east and off the highway with a few partitions on the upper level. Also a well for water was also dug but it was salty, never safe for drinking. At the outbreak of World War II when they were building, materials to make a home were very hard to come by. Metals, rubber, and other furnishings were scarce as the materials in them were used for the war effort. Wartime meant rationing of many building materials in Canada as well as rationing of foodstuffs like butter, meat and sugar, etc. Ration books containing stamps for these commodities can still be found in some homes today.[3] The Barrowmans soldiered on and managed to create a home on the property, nevertheless. In the living room, the most notable piece of furniture was the full size grand piano. Their focal point consisted of a fine fireplace containing a few, small, classical sculptures on the mantle.

James Barrowman was to become one of the three great male models for me and I owe him great respect and gratitude for how he enriched my life to this day.

A generous man and wife, Lois and James welcomed me to visit and stay for supper from the earliest days I can remember. One day when I was very young, the Barrowman family left their abode and headed to Yonge Street in North York to open an art and gift shop with a specialty in framing so that James could make a living. He rented his home to another family with about 4 children. A fire broke out in the garage and the firefighters were called to extinguish it. It wasn't long before that family were obliged to move out. Soon, like me, the original family came back to their original house with daughter Carol on weekends and holidays. Thus we became good friends. Dalzelle would soon move out on her own to start her own life and I had very little to do with Dalzelle.

James and Lois would arrive between 6:30 and 8:00 p.m. on a Friday night and start the supper. Corn cobs, potatoes and peas or carrots would follow with sausages or chicken which we all ate outside on a table overlooking the lake as the evening started its golden gleam. Every meal, no matter how big or small started with grace said by James and we all bowed our heads in reverence. James was a very religious man, always questioning people's actions and asking my views of current events. Lois, James, and Carol, were usually together there, for Carol lived at home with her parents. Dalzelle, the other twin had a different life and was a very different person than her sister. She married and had children in her early twenties.

On many occasions, another person would arrive for the weekend with them such as the Latvian born, Elmer Dambergs, who became a fundamentalist minister. James knew him through his art as Elmer was quite accomplished in watercolour, particularly. When I was 18, he painted my portrait while I sat on a log in the early twilight. I still have it. Elmer was also very religious and our discussions went on into the night. Sometimes Elmer would sit on a log with a 22 calibre rifle waiting to get rats as they scampered over the beach stones. I don't remember if he ever shot any though. Another time, the Reverend from his United Church in Toronto visited. Known for his sermons, in the United Church it didn't take long to realize this man was an eloquent preacher. His name was Rev. Crossley-Hunter of the Trinity United Church in North York. Then, from time to time, an art student, called Steven, who modelled for James's portraits would appear for the weekend. Models could be male or female and James painted them with an impressionistic style but he knew where each muscle and bone reflected or retreated from the light. His technical skills at anatomical structures were phenomenal and he could wield the brush with a such ease so that if you looked very closely at his work, there was almost nothing real visible. The viewer standing back about eight or ten feet, could see all the paint dobs and impressions worked magic on the viewer's eye. The image materialized magically before your eyes.

Barrowman Portrait in oil of the author when 18.

Watercolour portrait of author at 18 by Elmer Dambergs, House Guest

For James, art was the whole world and he could never get enough of talking about it. But art was a means through which he saw the morality of the world around him. It provided an opportunity to explore the meaning of art in a philosophical way. Always interested from a very young age in philosophy as I mentioned above, I couldn't wait until Friday night arrived and we could explore together what the essence of beauty was, or the difference between art and craft. Other times we could spend an evening discussing what a line or a hue on his canvas, newly painted, did for that particular painting. Most afternoons or evenings, James would be at his easel painting slowly and methodically from the faint charcoal sketch to the final framed masterpiece.

Oil on canvas "Farm at Madawaska" by James Barrowman

Over the breadth of the open field along the highway edge, James would stand his paintings for sale, usually on a Sunday afternoon so that motorist could stop and maybe appreciate his work enough to buy one. But his prices were in the $500 to $1000 range and there were few takers. To support the framed canvases upright, James erected steel supports which he fixed into the ground. Passing drivers could stop anywhere on the shoulder of the highway to inspect them.

On occasion, my grandmother would send a bouquet of her backyard flowers to the Barrowmans through me and they inevitably became the subject of a magnificent still life. However, my grandmother didn't appreciate art enough to purchase one. What was his style? It certainly was impressionistic. If you got too close there appeared to be nothing real there but as one stood back, his landscapes and portraits were as beautiful as if they had been painted by Renoir— at least to me, they were. Other times, the work took on a great abstract quality such as his *Sight of the Sound of Music* period of his painting. All the while, James would have a recording of *Madame Butterfly* or Verdi's *Don Giovanni* playing in the background as he painted away. These paintings were executed usually in the living room, his paints on a small table or on the grand piano. In the air, turpentine and linseed oil perfumed every room. I can smell it to this day and as I paint a little myself, my thoughts go back to those days recalling the images suggested by the scent of those two additives to oil paint. *En plain air* painting, was also a frequent sight for visitors to come upon as James made the local sights by the lake his subject matter.

Sometimes, I would be invited to breakfast after I showed up unannounced. Then began the morning meal with a reverent grace with the strong odour of kippers— that salty, strong dried Scottish herring dish which has been smoked for flavour. I never had them before or after I knew James but I did acquire a taste through him. James never cooked these though. He left his wife, Lois, whom he called Peggy, or Carol, his daughter, to prepare all the meals. In this respect, James was a typical father, husband and man of the early 20th century whose family members all had roles to play. It was thus in my own family where my grandfather was treated with utmost respect as head of the household. Mr. Barrowman's wife and daughter prepared nearly all the meals. If, while the opera music played out, Carol said a word to interrupt, James would erupt in anger for his daughter to cease at once. I often felt embarrassed for her to be berated so in front of me. Nevertheless, James was James and we all knew where we stood and what was expected and everyone unquestioningly followed the rules.

Photo shows the Barrowman family in the mid forties,
Lois, Carol, James and Dalzelle on their front lawn.

Lois Barrowman was a lovely lady, never criticizing anyone, nor finding fault. She was a good listener and had a wonderful laugh. Never easy to get to know, she appeared to be very in love with James and a great supporter of his work. Friendly and welcoming to whomever James had with him, she never complained but made his guests equally hers. Lois's nickname for James was a peculiar one — "McGeachie". When Peggy, his nick-name for her, called him that, it was an act of devotion. This name was chosen after a character on a popular radio program of the time.

On a warm summer afternoon, I came upon them by a couple of trees that stood atop the 20 foot high bank of shale which lined the edge of their property. Below lay the shingle beach. It soon became apparent that there was a heavy feeling in the air as board after board was being tossed down on the beach from a woodpile. The mood was evidently sad as I learned that these boards, now rotten and insect-ridden, were once to be the frame of a larger, more permanent home

— Lois and Jim's dream home. But it was not to be. Fortune did not shine on their aspirations and now the dream would never be realized. I felt very sad for them and especially Lois.

Never did I call them anything but Mr. and Mrs. Barrowman no matter how old I got. He called me Da-vid with a short a vowel sound accented on the first syllable as in Scottish. I liked the sound of it. Often he would refer to me as, "Young Feller."

Oil on canvas, "Lakeview Park", 1978, near
Oshawa, Ontario by James Barrowman.

One other memory I had of Mr. Barrowman is as follows: while driving with a back seat full of framed paintings one day in North York, a bus suddenly appeared coming from the right at a street intersection. James applied the brakes forcefully to avoid a collision and his paintings flew forward striking his head. He overcame the injury and fortunately after a brief hospital stay he recovered to paint another day.

Now Carol and I always had lots of fun too by the lake and by the shore. She came to my place and got to know my family equally as well as I knew hers. Often we did excursions to the railroad tracks or visited with other neighbouring kids, just hanging out or playing on the beach. We are still friends, though miles apart. Carol eventually married a farmer from the Kingston area, Sam McKane. They had one son, Jason who continued to take over his father's farming responsibilities while holding a full time job. Carol always worked in an office either in North York or later in the Kingston area until retirement. She also served in the Barrowman Art, the store owned by her parents on north Yonge Street in her earlier life.

Carol was a regular girl who cherished home life and she seemed to always be trying to make everyone around her happy. She was forever helping others and it was especially evident when relatives came to visit. No task was too much for her as she prepared a meal and made her guests and relatives comfortable. Always popular with children, Carol looked after all the children in the neighbourhood who showed up at her place. She was loving and kind, positive, and rarely complained. Whenever we went for a hike up the Trafalgar Road to the train tracks for example, she would carry the younger ones and hold their hands like a mother.

One time in the summer many years ago we took a walk up that road and along the tracks until we came to the trestle bridge that crossed Bronte Creek. There was Carol, Patty, and Jimmy Dewar, another little girl or two and myself. We dared to walk across the trestle having not seen a train there for at least a half hour as we trudged the track bed. About half way across, I said we had better turn back and we ran like crazy. Just then, before we got back to safety, a light from an engine approached in the distance to the west. We all ran praying to get to solid ground of the west bank. The train was about 300 yards away when we were all safe and we never did that again.

When James died suddenly of a heart attack in 1982, Lois lived alone on the property for a number of years. She cut the grass herself at first, then others helped. Lois took a volunteer job at the Presbyterian Church on New Street, checking the financial statements with her bookkeeping skills. Never did she let on how difficult life must have been for her during this time alone. Failing health made it mandatory for her to move to be near her daughter. Later, Lois found herself in Carol's Kingston area farm home. Ultimately, she took up residence in a retirement home nearby where she passed away. In 1990, Carol sold the property to the Halton Region to be a part of Burloak Waterfront Park. As stated earlier, this is the second earliest settled property in the now constituted park. The first was at the western end — the once-called Lakeshore Park nearest Hampton Heath.

Sadly, in scouring the internet,[4] I learned that over 950 of James Barrowman's paintings were destroyed in a fire in 1997. They were assessed at over a million dollars. A collector had acquired 900 of James Barrowman's paintings and only 37 of them were found after the fire. The claimant and her husband acquired them with a goal of purchasing Barrowman's complete work. However, the couple split up and the wife ended up in financial difficulties when her husband's wealth was not available anymore. The insurance company claimed that the house was deliberately set on fire. The court found for the claimant, a Mrs. Sagl. She was deemed a hoarder by the judge, and thus believed not capable of destroying her own belongings. The CHUBB company, on appeal, was forced to award the claimant a settlement of over $4,500,000 plus costs and interest. $1,005,000 was for the Barrowman collection. What a sad loss! I was totally shocked and very sad to see how James's life's work had gone up in smoke. Thank goodness it wasn't his complete work. This case ultimately was appealed to the Supreme Court of Ontario and was settled in 2015 as described above. Thus it was that a dear family that once occupied this beautiful property in what is now a public park faced the reality of James's paintings and his legacy largely destroyed. I have trouble talking about it.

2

The Cantell and Furdos Families

Next door, Reginald Cantell and his wife, Martha, left Hamilton to retire on the shores of Lake Ontario in 1941. Apparently, they owned a summer home at Pointe au Baril in the cottage country of Ontario. They were made aware of the property for sale on the Great Lake by a one time machinist for P.B. Yates Company which was Cantell's employer. That machinist was James Barrowman, first buyer of land in that eastern strip. The Cantells were wealthy by any standard and built themselves a raised ranch frame house about 30 feet from the water's edge. Their property frontage measured about 200 feet and bordered on his colleague James Barrowman's property. Barrowman, after all, worked at P. B. Yates Company until he had an accident with one of the machines. Reginald and Martha also purchased a tract of land on the north side of Lakeshore opposite their own place. This they later sold off in pieces over several years. The land was between the Pig and Whistle Inn and the Hill residence.

Whether the Cantells were millionaires or not, I do not know but they were reputed to be. They prepared their property for development by fortifying the waterfront shore with armour stone boulders about four feet long. They sloped the embankment behind the armour stone to prevent erosion and placed cement-filled oil drums on the slope to nearly the top. Their bank along the shore was about twenty feet high above the water. Next, a boathouse on the bank and a pier about 25 to 30 feet was erected in concrete extending into the lake. But Cantell didn't stop there, he had a steel frame built in the water to hoist his motor boat out of the lake and into the boat-house on a track. There it would be safe from the often very rough waters of this great lake.

View in today's park of the former Cantell/
Furdos and Barrowman properties.

I do not remember seeing them use their motor boat very often — maybe half a dozen times. In the month of April one year I do recall seeing Mr. Cantell and a passenger head off for a ride going east. He wore a parka for the cold wind at that time of year. The boathouse, pier, and sling device lasted for many years into the late 50's and early sixties. However, the boathouse gradually deteriorated and fell into pieces. Eventually, the pier was knocked over and buried beneath the waves after frequent torrential storms. Today only the armour stone and oil barrels remain and can be found if one looks carefully along the new additions of armour stone put their by the region for reinforcement. The whole length of the water-front property at the back was planted with willow trees which gracefully draped themselves over the water each summer. As a kid I spent many hours sailing rafts past the property and running barefoot over these giant boulders. I rarely ever saw the Cantells outside. The rocks extended about eight feet onto Barrowman's property next door and there we would jump off the rocks into the lake. It is where I actually learned to swim.

Sometime around 1951 an aluminum antenna sprouted up

DAVID WOODWARD

from the Cantell residence. This was the new television technology that brought pictures into the home all across North America and perhaps the world. I had not seen a television set by then and remember staring at the antenna wondering how pictures could be transmitted through the air and be received this way. I was about a year later that a great aunt of mine in Toronto actually purchased a TV and I became hooked. On Danforth Avenue in Toronto where I went to school, some appliance shops advertised their sets for sale in the windows. In the early evenings my friends and I would head down to watch a show through the window. "You Bet your Life " with Groucho Marx was my favourite then. But it was Cantell who first drew my attention to this new invention that I could only imagine then, never having seen one when I first saw his antenna.

A long wooden white picket fence lined the roadside edge of the Cantell property. The grass behind was cut by a local farmer from about half a mile east of there. His name was George Furdos. He was hired to care for the property and I often watched as he put out the hose. Such large front lawn required an extensive hose which was placed so that several creeping sprinkler heads would crawl along the length covering the extent in the hot summer days. Years later I found one these sprinklers tossed into the lake and took it to my grandfather for his use. It still worked.

The Cantell boathouse and pier, now long gone due to the lake ferocity

Years went by and in 1954 the Cantells sold their property and George and Julie Furdos were the lucky ones to purchase it. Still a farmer, he chose to remain on his farm and rent out the property which had a second small building and garage by now, #5478. It was located to the right of the main house, #5478A. Furdos's tenants were the Puhlman family whom I got to know when they visited my grandparents occasionally. They had a beautiful young daughter with sparkling blue eyes. After the farm to the west on the lakeshore was sold for a development now called Newport Village, the Furdos couple were happy to have been assured that their former farm land would be memorialized in the new development. It was intended that a street would be named for them called Furdos Lane. However, a bureaucratic error seems to have occurred. Furdos Lane did not appear and several years after all the new homes were sold, the new owners refused to change the name of their residential streets to accommodate a promise made long before. Over the years, after several discussions at Burlington Council and in the newspapers, Julie's conversation occasionally betrayed a bitter feeling about this, and that I can understand.

In 1976, the first female mayor of Burlington was elected, Mary Munro. Making a name for herself, Mary led the Burlington Save the Lakeshore Association for several years before being elected to Council in 1973. She came up with a plan to save the lakeshore from development, arguing the case at an Ontario Municipal Board Hearing in June of 1973. Accessible land was getting nearly impossible along the 5 miles of easterly property that belonged to the new Town of Burlington since amalgamation in 1958. Her plan was to have the City of Burlington acquire land in the vicinity of the Burloak Drive to Hampton Heath area as it became available. No plans were made to expropriate. When reading of this in the newspaper, a hastily-called meeting was arranged by the Puhlman family, Furdos's tenants, on their back patio. The landowners along their strip gathered there to hash out what we could do about it. It was the only time I was ever in that home until sold later in the 90's. I went to this meeting where we all discussed the oncoming threat. It was then that I realized that I might never be able to live on my grandfather's land sometime in the future. The Critchleys, Ealeses,

Koleffs, and Puhlmans were there, at the meeting. I do not remember any grand plans to do anything about it arising from the discussion. We all at the meeting went back home and worried about how long we had to remain owners of these properties. In the end no-one was ever forced to sell. It was over 30 years before the plans to develop the park were underway. The first plan was revealed in September 1986. It included a miniature Lake Ontario being centered in the park with a miniature Niagara Falls showing all landmarks around the lake. A children's Centre was to be located in the original Cantell house. After I sold my property, the Halton Region started to protect the existing properties from further erosion. River rocks were seeded along the length of the park where needed for a width of about 75 feet. Stairways to the beach and water were placed in three locations as they are today. The original plan was deemed far too costly and thus impossible. It was supplanted by the present plan as outlined in the map at the back of this book. The property came up for sale piece by piece until the last parcel was bought from Margaret Landsborough in 2014. In 2016/17 a gazebo near the swings and playground was erected and the long pathway opened the park to anyone who wanted to enjoy the new development. Further and final plans will be implemented in 2018 when the park is completed. Already I have noticed an increasing number of area residents and passers-by stopping for a respite or walk along the shore. The gazebo and playground are very popular as well as the beaches.

Over the years, George and his wife Julie Furdos moved into their lakeshore property and the Puhlman family moved away. There was another tenant in the remaining building on the property as well. I never got to meet him until about 2014 while I visited the new parkland one day and happened to strike up a conversation with him. Furdos sold their lakeshore farm in between, bought another one north near Walker's Line and lived there until George had a car accident leaving his face badly scarred. It was then that they sold their farm up Walker's Line and moved to the former Cantell property.

After I sold my property to the Region of Halton in 1988, there were occasional meetings held with residents attending to discuss park development. I attended several of these. Julie Furdos and Margaret Landsborough were there too. I had inherited the property in 1985 and was not allowed to do anything with the existing building to enhance it for my needs; hence I sold it to the Regional Municipality of Halton in 1989. At those meetings, held at the Pig and Whistle building, the councillor from Burlington, Mike Wallace, took notes and we brainstormed what we wanted such a park to look like. The main ideas consisted of leaving the area as natural as possible with shale banks, stone beaches, and trees for the birds and shore life. It has remained so until this day awaiting several million dollars of investment to make it a continuous park, not one with divisions of property lines still visible. Over those many years property values rose dramatically along Lakeshore Road. I paid property tax of about $600 annually in 1988 and my neighbour Margaret was charged about $9000 when she sold. Her property was only slightly larger with a modest home with no basement. Her father added a room on the back from the kitchen and built a root cellar beneath a small part of it.

Sometime in the new century, George Furdos became infirm and had to live in the long term care retirement residence at Burloak and New Street until his death. Julie also became infirm around her mid nineties and she joined her husband at the same location until her death July 12, 2014. She was 98 years old. I had last seen her when she had a garage sale at the lakeshore home presided over by a nephew just before she sold. Such is the story of this parcel of land that once was a private home for several families over fifty years.

3

The Eales Couple: A Londoner and a Swede

What do you do when you have a married couple living next to you who are not sociable at all? This childless couple were Hedwig and James W. Eales. Hedwig must have been an attractive young woman in her youth, I imagine. She had blonde hair with a reddish tinge and lovely blue eyes. She came from Sweden and spoke with a very thick Swedish accent. That is, she spoke occasionally, but usually not at all. On a rare occasion, my grandparents, one or the other, sometimes both, would be out tending to the garden by the Eales's fence. An exchange of conversation between them would ensue once in a while at the same time they were pruning, raking, or digging in the garden. It was as though Hedwig needed an excuse to get to talk to her neighbours. I always thought that Mrs. Eales did not like government, especially the municipal level of government for her conversation usually would be about her property and taxes. I also remember her often talking about Swedish massage, something she was good at. Jim's accent was as thick as his wife's but he spoke with a London cockney accent, of course. I think I only heard him talk to us on five or six occasions for he was not a friendly man, at least not to his neighbours. Hedwig, his wife, he called, "Wig."

This former Londoner was said to be a Dr. Barnardo Home Boy. As an orphan he may have been sent to Canada by the famous Dr. Barnardo from London to give him a chance for a better life. Many Barnardo boys were transported to homes in Canada for a type of adoption which usually meant they became farm labourers for their room and board. Many were not treated well at all. If Jim was one of those orphan children, he doesn't seem to show up on any published lists, at least as far as I have been able to research. It seems that as husband and wife, they were admitted to the United States in about 1928 and lived in Chicago, Illinois. His occupation was listed as radio technician. Apparently he had lived in Toronto before this from 1927 to 1928 and went back and forth over the border several times. At one time he worked in a piano factory in Oshawa. They were listed as having little money in the records of Ancestry.com but the previous information came from this modern source.

In Burlington, Jim had a small shop on James street in the middle of the block between John and Brant, on the south side. It would have been in the long time designated Elizabeth Interiors building. The sign on the front said, "Burlington Radio - Repairs." Inside, where I went only once as a child, there seemed to be numerous used items for sale and the odd radio could be seen on a table or shelf. It didn't look very prosperous. We all thought that the business was a second hand shop selling used items. Some people in the town had a nickname for Mr. Eales. They called him, "Slippery Eales." This I heard from a Burlington downtown resident when we were eating ice cream in the Lakeside Dairy on Brant Street. We had told our table neighbour that we lived on the lakeshore next to James Eales, the radio store proprietor. Although hearsay, nevertheless, it was an interesting moniker and one my family didn't forget.

It was rumoured that Hedwig had the money that built their Cape Cod style red brick house with two garages on the side. At the back was a flagstone patio. The highlight of their landscaping was a beautiful blue spruce in the centre of the front lawn. In the Christmas season, this tree was decorated with oversize light bulbs in multi colours and it was pretty sight. The house was still under construction when my grandfather purchased the lot next door. Their lot was a good size — over one hundred feet frontage along the highway and backed by Lake Ontario. There were a lot of maple trees and some Austrian pines lining the driveway ending at the two car garage.

View of the Kolassa farm home today across from Critchley's and Eales's.

Against our fence Mr. Eales had a small one-roomed cottage placed which was about eight feet square. Sometime later, they built a sitting area on the bank of the lake that led down some steps to the lake bottom. Finally, along our fence also ran a driveway paved with crushed black cinders. All in all, the property had a good aspect and seemed to be large for just two people.

Now this couple were very strange characters. They made my grandparents' lives a living hell. I really don't know how it all got started as my grandfather said, "They were friendly enough when we bought the adjoining piece of land to their property." But the Ealeses soon got kind of nasty when they learned that our house was going to be closer to the highway than theirs was situated. The fence between us and them was constructed of barb wire the top facing over to our side because of a bend near the top of the posts. The fence was all wire. In the chapter about the Critchley family, the reader can see how life was so hellish for my family during the years of construction leading to their permanent retirement next to this couple. Therefore I will not repeat that part of the story here.

My grandfather got around to building himself a work shed adjacent to the smaller Eales' shed. One day when they arrived out from our home in Toronto to continue building their house, a new addition to the Eales's property had been set up. It was a dog kennel for two Irish setters, named Duke and Duchess. After all, James was a Londoner by birth. The two dogs lived in the pen (kennel), almost exclusively. When anyone went near the pen which had been placed right at our fence line, they barked... and barked.. . and barked. Duchess would yap away and leap in circles at the same time, as if she were behaving strangely. It is not difficult to see neighbourliness was not a priority here. How horrible it was when we had visitors to take them down to the lake and had to walk by the yelping of the dogs! The noise was enough to drive us inside. The dogs didn't stop until we went in. Our neighbours never tried to quiet them or move them. It was as though the dogs were out there to annoy us. And it lasted for years until the dogs died and were not replaced. Unfortunately this went on until one died and then the other dog passed on. We were not sorry. Although we had a small pekingese dog of our own and would never harm a pet no matter how awful they were.

Now in the early days, the Ealeses had a few visitors on a weekend when we were building the house. On one occasion I can remember there was a loud yelling in the drive as their visitors were leaving in their car. James's voice was heard in his cockney best to say, "Next time you come, bring a bl—dy roast of beef." They never came back. Neither did anyone else it seemed. I don't believe Hedwig or Jim encouraged visitors anyway. Yet in the 50's one day in the early summer, a sign post hanging on an L-shaped pipe support was erected at the end of the driveway by the highway. "Lakeshore Lodge OVERNIGHT GUESTS", it read. Our neighbours were taking in visitors to make a few dollars but nothing was said about bed and breakfast. What they charged, we never knew. This went on for a few years only in the summer. Guests were allowed to go down to the lake to swim off the cement slab there. But few actually took advantage of the opportunity. The lake was too cold, I guess. But it was almost never too cold for me or my friends.

A strange point of note should be mentioned here. Mrs. Eales had family in Sweden and every once in a while one or the other of her sisters or her brother would visit for a few days. The brother told us that he was not allowed to stay in the main house but in the leaky-roofed shed which was unheated. How peculiar that they took into their home overnight guests but relegated the only family they had to the outdoor shed. We could never understand who would treat family like that.

In the year 1957, Queen Elizabeth II visited Ottawa as the Canadian Head of State. That is the only time the monarch has opened the Canadian Parliament as the personification of the Canadian Crown. John Diefenbaker was newly elected Prime Minister and he invited the Queen to preside over her Canadian Parliament, one of her most important duties, constitutionally speaking. This duty she carries out in the United Kingdom regularly at the beginning of each session — the Opening of Parliament. The occasion was historic and magnificent with the red coated Mounties riding as escort to the landau carrying the Queen and Prince Philip. As a backdrop, Ottawa's red maples and orange-yellow tree canopy made a stunning backdrop to the autumn pageant. This was the year that James W. Eales fell and broke his back at the bottom of a ladder he had used to get down to the lake bottom. It happened in August 1957. Their previous steps and structure had collapsed into the lake by then. The second rung from the top broke and down he fell. Unfortunately, at the bottom were some large rocks and James fell on one of them breaking his back. In spite of how we had been treated by this man, my grandfather and I assisted the ambulance medical people in getting him to the ambulance from the bottom of his lot. There was a vacant field two lots west of us and the ambulance drove down the empty field as far as possible. Four of us walked to the place where James was lying by the water and we carried the stretcher back to the ambulance about 250 feet. The rest of the summer James spent in Toronto Western hospital for treatment.

During his absence, I was asked by Hedwig if I would paint the wrought iron fence sections that ran across the front of her boundary by the highway. These had been newly purchased from some estate sale. I did this for $15.00 and she wrote me a cheque. James came home sometime later. He approached my grandfather at the fence with two glasses and a bottle of wine offering him a drink. Then he told my grandfather that he was a changed man since his fall. It was not to last. In October, that year, after the celebrations and pageantry in Ottawa were concluded I waited for the bus to Toronto. Then the Eales couple stopped at the gate and asked if I was going to Toronto and they offered me a ride to Sunnyside near the Humber River. I got in the car and went with them that far, taking a streetcar or two to get home from there. I hardly remember the conversation in the car but it was the only time I remember them being talkative and congenial. James did comment on the Ottawa pomp and circumstance as being better than in England, I remember. But this expression of warmth and neighbourliness was not to last as previously noted. I was fifteen years old in grade ten.

The only other strange things I remember about James was that he had a pick-up truck, yellow and old. Visitors often drove up to the house and James would go to his truck and take something out of it giving it to the visitor who then drove off. I never learned what the exchange consisted of.

Many years later, he started yelling at me to cut off branches overhanging his driveway from my grandfather's maple tree. I told him it wasn't my tree and if he wanted to he could cut them off himself. This soon degenerated into a personal attack on me in front of my visiting girlfriend which infuriated me so much that I never had any words with him again.

A view of the westerly edge of the Eales's property
where stairs have been erected to the beach.

Mrs. Eales ended up passing away due to cancer. James, much later, was heard moaning on the back patio by my mother one day. She called an ambulance and he had a broken knee cap which took some time to heal. Finally, in 1980 he was picked up off the patio again having suffered a heart attack and being alone, there was no one to get to him soon enough and he died. Their home was acquired by the Halton Region for the proposed Burloak park in about 1983.

Now as I look back I feel sorry for these neighbours in a way. They had such a poor social existence — so different from all our other neighbours. I wonder if we had tried to be more outgoing toward them, would they have responded in kind? In light of what we experienced with them it was not something we thought possible at the time.

4

My Perfect World —
The Critchley-Woodward Family

Growing up along Lake Ontario in the 40's and 50's was my paradise and refuge. Growing up in Toronto in those same years provided me a rich base of experiences and a wonderful education. Born in Toronto in the Danforth district at Albany Clinic between Broadview and Pape Avenues I was fortunate to live in Toronto in those decades and half of the 60's. Our home was a few houses inside the city near the boundary of East York. We lived north of "the Danforth" in a corner house. I was born the only child of Aleda and Raymond Woodward. My world from the time I was nine months old consisted really of two distinct environments: the city and the country. These two separate worlds gave me what few other children ever had — the possibility of endless rural holidays and the routine of urban life with all its rich cultural opportunities at my fingertips. Having no siblings, I had to make my own fun most of the time. I did this in the rural environment exploring the lakeshore area and visiting the homes and people along the shore.

In Toronto I played on the street with neighbour friends until the street lights came on. As far as friends of my own age were concerned, there were only a few I played with in what is now Burlington They were the Tomlinson boys, the Barrowman girls, the younger children of the Kowal family, and the nephew of the Noseworthys, Bill Hubbard, who lived in Hamilton. He visited his aunts frequently on the north side of the Lakeshore Road. We spent a lot of time at the farm of

John Kolassa where he let us help with chores, ride the tractor to get supplies to the house from the barn, and we often visited with the animals. By some chance, Bill also grew up to be a teacher and when I moved to my first house in east Burlington, he was my neighbour across the street. Starting out in elementary grades, he decided to move to the second-ary panel and taught geography and history and other subjects at Nelson High School until his retirement.

The moonlight scene that stole my grandparents' hearts. It inspired a new dream for them.

It was six months after I screamed into this world that my grandparents, Fred and Martha Critchley went for a fateful drive. That September or October of 1942 would change all our lives forever. Fred, my grandfather, was approaching retirement within five years and with my grandmother, they enjoyed leisurely drives east and west of Toronto on the week-ends. They were looking for possible places to put up their feet. This time they went west in their 1940 Oldsmobile coupe. It was their last new car and one day it would be mine. This particular clear, moonlit evening, on their way back to the city, a harvest moon rose over Lake Ontario near Bronte Ontario. This was about 30 miles west of Toronto.

What a spectacular orange sphere it was! They stopped the car by the side of the King's Highway 2 to walk through a grassy field at the edge of the steep shale bank. Out over the water, a trail of shimmering orange from the glowing orb cast such a spell on them that they couldn't even talk for many minutes while they took in such beauty. In a while, shuffling through lengthy, knee-high grasses, they stumbled over a submerged sign advertising land for sale. It carried the Toronto solicitor's phone number.[5] Someone had knocked it down.

It only took a few days but the couple found $425 cash in their meagre savings to buy a lot 300 feet deep to the lake and fifty feet wide. Such a lot was gigantic compared to the 20 feet wide house they had in Toronto. This was to be their retirement home and they would build it together. Such a property could be maintained by an older man in his senior years. Soon over the weekends to follow, they would drive out to Nelson Township and start construction.

Now Fred was a carpenter, joiner, and cabinet maker from Oldham, Lancashire, England who sailed for Canada in 1902. He arrived at Halifax, Pier 21, bound for Toronto. Indeed, he apprenticed in Oldham and Blackpool where he was one of the builders of the Blackpool Tower dance floor. Martha, or Nellie, as she was called by her friends, (Martha Ellen Gladys Tasker) emigrated from Redhill, Surrey, England. She arrived in Toronto in 1908 or 09 after a short stint as a domestic in Jonquiere, Quebec. They met in a movie theatre on Danforth Avenue sometime after 1911. Although they boarded in separate houses on the same street they had not met before. She, with her merry laughter, and he, with his clear, bright blue eyes fell in love after meeting at a cinema to which they each went alone. In June 1912, a few months after the Titanic disaster, three days after she turned 18, Fred and Nellie were married. But Fred was 28 years old. Their marriage lasted over 65 years. They managed a short honeymoon by train to Niagara Falls.

In time, I started to accompany them to their dream home location on the weekends. I was born in 1942, the year they bought the land. My parents lived in my grandparents' Toronto home at that time and it was easy for me to be looked after by my mother's parents. Later, when they moved out to the rural location, my parents stayed behind and rented the house from them. The house in Toronto still stands a long block north of the Danforth. It was purchased new in 1919 when Granddad returned from the Great War. He served his new country nearly four years overseas in the trenches of France and Belgium: Ypres, Amiens, Arras, Mons, Passchendale, and Vimy, to name a few battles in which he fought with the 38th Battalion.

Sergeant Fred Critchley writes home a letter to his
wife Ellen from overseas in the Great War

Fred never really wanted to go to war, I am sure. He was a
peaceful man, compassionate, and always wanted to get along
with everyone he met. I cannot remember him getting angry
or saying unkind remarks to people. He treated his family with
the utmost respect as we did him. I have a difficult time imag-
ining him in assault mode with the enemy. However, at this
time, jobs were difficult to find in his trade. He was a loyal supporter of his country and empire and he knew his duty was to
enlist in his new country's armed forces and go back overseas
to do his part in the effort to restore France and Belgium to
their rightful territories.

Training was at Niagara Camp in Niagara-on-the-Lake. Bell
tents were erected in the fields adjacent to the Festival Theatre
of today. It was across the road from Fort George. Soon he
was obliged to use his woodworking skills as a carpenter and
joiner to construct wooden floors in the tents. The floors
were to keep the men dry and free from dampness. On a few

occasions, the wives of the men were invited to visit their men a the camp as a morale booster before they were shipped overseas. As an NCO, (non-commissioned officer), of the rank of sergeant, Fred was allowed to take Nellie to the NCO mess for dinner on these few occasions. Nellie boarded a train from Union Station with a few of her close friends whose husbands were at the camp as well and headed off for a day to remember. She put on her large picture hat, her silken-blue blouse, and white gloves, with long navy skirt and button shoes. I think she would have made Fred a happy man to welcome her, if even for a day.

Later she would retire to a house on the main street that offered overnight accommodation. The house there still stands on the main street north of the Royal George Theatre. Whenever we visited the town she would point out this building to her family with a bit of a tear in her eye. The next morning she would stand on Queen Street hoping to catch a glimpse of her husband as he passed by on parade – a march of ten to fifteen miles along the roads to Queenston. Then alas, she and her friend would get to the railway station for the ride home. I never asked her how she got there. There are so many questions that come to mind after it's too late!

He came home without harm and started rebuilding the Toronto home he had just newly bought. Better quality hardwood floors he installed of oak, maple, and walnut inlaid designs which were set into the floors. Stained glass windows over his beautiful wooden mantle, intricately carved and trimmed were his focus for the living and dining rooms. Two sunrooms, top and bottom were added at the back, and a garage for two cars. Martha's parents, Thomas and Mary Ann went to live there with them in that house until their deaths. In 1918 — he from Spanish flu, and in 1924, she, from a kidney disease. Therefore, with all this construction background, Fred began to build his house by the lake when near retirement

Their property was open and airy inside being on a corner. How I loved that house! It was fun to grow up there in east Toronto. As a child I walked to 3 schools from kindergarten to Grade thirteen and later attended Toronto Teachers' College a short few blocks from my house. I walked there and back also. In between, I studied political science and economics at the University of Toronto, Trinity College. In 1966 I moved full time to my grandparents' home when I was 24 to become a Burlington teacher.

We would drive to "Bronte" and back each weekend and I can barely remember those early experiences. However, when I was four several vivid memories crowd my mind: stringing up wire fences on each side of the property with two rows of barbed wire at the top, and the building of a gated picket fence along the highway at the front, west side. Actually, there were two gates: a wide one for the driveway and a small one for the path that led to the house on the east side connecting the gate to the front porch. The pathway consisted of flag stones placed a few inches apart and wound around a crooked cut-leaf soft maple tree about 30 years old. The driveway was covered with crushed cinders and we rolled the length of it back and forth with a water-filled roller to pack it down. To round out the improvements, a shipment of spruce trees arrived from the Agricultural College in Guelph provided at no cost for a wind break. At least that is what I remember being told. These were planted along the sides of the property in front on the fences and another row at the other side of the drive to the garage. Some of these are still surviving in the new Burloak Waterfront Park. All in all, it was a small but picturesque bungalow with 6 rooms, a basement, bathroom, and cold cellar under the front stoop.

Our Toronto home in the east end of Toronto in what is Greektown today. This home, Fred bought new on returning from WWI in 1919.

DAVID WOODWARD

All the wood for construction was purchased from the mills at Halliday's and Nicholson's in the Maple Avenue area of Burlington. Costing in total less than $1000, the wood was such that you cannot get today and included gum wood baseboards, ash for the floors and thick cedar wood for closets. Bob Imber was the plumber from Port Nelson who installed the bathroom fixtures. On some weekends, my grandfather's work friends, who were old WWI buddies came out from Toronto to help with framing of the house. We had great picnic lunches and lots of table talk about the old days. Horace Mountain, born in the Channel Islands was the most faithful helpmate. During the war he was a motorcycle driver for relaying messages at the front. He had a glass eye and his wife was disabled by a stroke at 38 years old. How she could read the tea leaves in a teacup! The way the leaves lined up when the liquid was drained from inside the cup, supposedly was the harbinger of good or ill fortune. Horace went on to be a lifelong visitor to our house and a wonderful friend.

Horace Mountain, (left) and Fred Critchley by the Lake in 1959

Another regular visitor on weekends throughout the later years was Walter Duck and his wife Ethel. A QSM, (Quarter Sergeant Major) from the Boer War, Walter lived a few blocks form Fred's Toronto house. He served in the 35th and 38th Battalions for all the Great War years with my grandfather. The stories they would tell about the war were infrequent but all of them concerned funny things that happened. Rarely was there anything said about the gore, muck, and horror. There was the lady in Belgium where my grandfather was billeted who pressed into his hand a small ivory crucifix with a gem at the cross brace. He credited that with saving his life when he jumped out of a watery shell hole to be stretcher bearer. When he reached the fallen lad a live shell bombed out his former shelter place and blew up all his comrades. The crucifix was for carrying the Belgian lady's feather bed out of her burning house. Though my grandfather was not a religious man he still revered that item as a talisman, proudly showing it to family members from time to time. He believed it saved his life.

One weekend I cannot forget, we arrived to find the cellar foundation of the house flooded with rain water. The tarpaulin covering it to keep out rain had been pried off in several locations so that water was about six inches deep and had to be bailed out taking the whole weekend. There were no machines at our disposal to do this. This kind of incident happened several times. Who would do this? Why would they do such a thing? How discouraging and scary to me as a young boy!

Worse still occurred many months later when the frame was up and the windows in. Our shock came when we discovered a huge granite boulder thrown through the window onto the living room floor. Shards of glass were everywhere. Even the foundation plants had been pulled out by the roots and tossed about a dry stone wall which was part of the landscaping design. A call to the local constabulary resulted in Nelson Township's constable, Harvey Hunt, appearing on the scene to investigate. Constable Hunt was a very tall, strong man, firm of voice. He attempted to reassure us that they would get the culprit. I was scared of this man until he reached in his pocket and gave a dime and a nickel and then I warmed up to him. Harvey later became a chief of police here. Years later, my wife, a registered nurse would work alongside his daughter Shirley, at the Joseph Brant Hospital for over 32 years. She and my family are still great friends.

Fred and Martha Ellen Gladys Critchley on the
occasion of their 65th anniversary in 1977.

There existed about 500 feet west of our boundary, a
private park owned by Sam Bolus. It is now the seven acres
that became an early private park at the west end of today's
Burloak Waterfront Park. We used to get water from his well to
fill our five gallon thermos. Mr. Bolus told us that our neighbours on the eastern fence had been dining in his restaurant
just prior to the vandalism and he overheard them talking to
each other about whether the "bogeyman would be around
tonight." But there was no proof of anyone vandalizing our
property so we just kept gritting our teeth each time we took
the trip to the new house.

At one further instance the window glass was shattered as if
hit by a crow bar and my grandmother picked up some broken
shards and placed them beneath the soil around the roots of
the cedars that graced the front porch. The following weekend
the cedars had been torn out and the neighbour next door
was seen with bandages on both hands. But no one was able to

say we had found our man. Someone didn't want anybody, not us anyway, living there. Or so it seemed. In any case, Granddad told him that the police knew who was doing this and they were going to get him. From that time on the vandalism stopped. As a young child I was often scared when I came with them to the house in the country but my grandparents were quite reassuring and protective and my fear gradually subsided. Nan was a strong person with a strong personality, where Fred was mild and mellow. Nan fervently took positions and stood her ground in interactions with both family and others. She stood by her man by helping him dig holes for fence posts, picked up rocks, planted trees, and rolled the cinder driveway. She helped lay the flagstones and paint the raw boards and walls in her developing home. Always a good cook, everyone was well-cared for during her whole life. She did all this and went to work at an outside job as well.

Back view of the Critchley bungalow we called Covertside.

Arriving in the cold winter months from Toronto on Saturday morning was no fun. The furnace had to be lit and we huddled by the heat duct vents with our coats on while sipping a cup of hot tea. We were English after all. A good cup of hot tea is always the answer to stress and discomfort. When it came time for my bath, it was down the basement in the laundry tubs during the summers with a pot of boiling water mixed with rain water from the catch barrel outside by the down-spout. How I hated this! Soon I put up enough protests that they stopped doing this. The rain barrel often had mosquito wrigglers and they were not what I wanted to be immersed in! This was before we had a proper well from which we could get potable drinking and bath water.

That's when I learned what a divining rod was. This was a small branch broken from the giant willow tree from a nearby vacant lot. It had a slight downward curve shaped with a fork at the end. My grandfather held the fork end against his body, one in each hand, and walked forward with it looking for movement of the branch. Suddenly the curve moved toward the ground at the far end which pointed to the spot where one could dig a well. Water!!! Sure enough, that's where the well was dug by a professional crew and round concrete tiles were placed inside. It was located on the east side of the house near the chimney. That well served us many years and had a pump handle at the top of it. Inside the basement was attached an electric pump with a tank to draw water off into a tank and the run of copper pipes that led to the taps in the house. No more huge picnic thermoses to lug back from the pump at Bolus's restaurant for us. I honestly remember how tasty that well water was, and how cool and fresh it was in those early days. Everyone along the Burloak Park strip of land had a well on their property. In Chapter 5, the reader will see that an older well had been dug about 100 feet from this one in the early 1800's. Settlers had been living for generations in this new province of Ontario, using the traditional divining rod as a way of finding water pioneered over centuries in Europe. Now it would probably be laughed at. For us it worked like science and I was so proud that I had such a smart grandfather.

Rafting on Lake Ontario, David and the girl who became his wife

When the family bungalow was finally finished, it was time to move in and we rented a moving truck from Toronto to load up with the furniture and set off. I was allowed to stand up in the truck amidst the furniture all the way to Burlington and hope that the pieces didn't fall on top of me. One door on the truck did not completely close. I did not remember whether I was alone in the back of the truck or not but I suspect not. It is hard to imagine anyone allowing that these days. It was then, in 1946, that my grandfather was near to retirement from Christie Street Hospital in Toronto. His job was making children's toys and furniture for Vetcraft Industries. From that time on my most frequent travel to this enchanted place was by Gray Coach Bus Lines. It stopped wherever one wanted to get off or on and wound its way through the towns and villages along the lakeshore to the Bay and Dundas terminal. When we bought a ticket we asked for a ticket to Innville. It was probably named for the location of the Pig and Whistle Inn at the corner of the town line and Lakeshore Road. Burloak Drive is today the town line between Nelson and Trafalgar Townships. It was called Trafalgar Line in the days of which I write. Innville was a stop listed on the ticket itself. For nearly twenty years I caught the bus in this way nearly every weekend and for school holidays. A street sign in the Great Lakes Boulevard

DAVID WOODWARD

development recalls the name Innville today.

My parents came out for holidays for a week or two at a time in the summers and they took the bus for many weekends too. We did not own a car like my grandparents. My name, Woodward, from my father, traces back to Cornwall England in the early 1800's. The Woodwards married into loyalist descendants who were from the founding families of Kingston. Others married late loyalists who emigrated from Holland to New Amsterdam, New York. Ancestors from the Rhine and Saxony were soldiers in the Battle of Saratoga, New York, during the American Revolution and emigrated to Canada for land. Thus my family goes back in America to about 1610.

I went to school in Toronto for all my school years: Wilkinson Public School, Earl Grey Senior public School, Riverdale Collegiate Institute, and later Trinity College, University of Toronto. During all those years I followed the habit I just mentioned. Work cutting grass and helping on the farm on the north side of the road was always available. It was a grand life for a boy in the fifties. I shall elaborate these events and memories in coming chapters as I relate the characters who didn't really know they resided in a place the bus line called Innville. The Gray Coach line presumably named the area Innville after the Pig and Whistle Inn. I have never found that name to be recorded anywhere else to denote the area but I considered choosing it for the title of this book because it was an official place on a major bus line schedule. All my young life I purchased a ticket to Innville to my second home. Although no one in the area ever claimed to live in Innville. One could catch the bus or get at any spot for about 2000 feet at this so-called destination. This stop consisted of the area east of the Pig and Whistle in Trafalgar Township to several hundred feet east of Shoreacres Road, the next "stop" on the Lakeshore bus line.

5

Home Life at Covertside and a Great Discovery

Living through the days and nights at Covertside, our country home in those days, was fairly quiet and predictable for the most part. Each day would start with getting up and having a quick wash followed by breakfast of cereal or eggs and toast. Sometimes we would make a larger meal and have bacon or sausages and pancakes with it but mostly this meal was very simple. Of course tea was included and rarely coffee. My mother used to like to lie outside on a sun cot and read a book while tanning. I used to quickly go to the park area nearby and swim off the part which is now a paved promontory that extends out into the lake near the children's playground. We, nearly daily, started swimming there where my local friends would meet together. We would dive underwater looking for a white stone, then lie on a picnic bench with our towel to dry off. After several hours of this we would walk along the beach gathering stones that had beautiful colours. Sometimes beach glass that was ground smooth was our quest, or driftwood. Then we would all go home for lunch at our respective homes. A sandwich and/or soup or spaghetti would be sufficient setting us up with enough energy for the afternoon. The farm across the road would be our target and we could always find something of interest to do there. We never asked permission and John Kolassa usually let us roam around his farm. Other times we would go to the Pig and Whistle rocks area to swim. Inner tubing was fun and so was building rafts with logs and driftwood as they washed ashore on the two local beaches.

My grandparents usually went about their tasks of laundering, making puddings or pies or shopping at the local grocery store in Skyway Plaza. Granddad had a tool shed where he liked to make and restore furniture and otherwise repair things. He made many items for the house and garden there. It was his special place. In the afternoon he always had a lie down for his "forty winks." He always credited that for his long life, living to 95. My grandmother, Nan, I called her, had her special chores. She actually starched clothing and even pillow slips. How did she find the energy to be always preparing puddings, pies, sometimes jams and jellies or pickled onions? In the end she lived a long life also, passing away at 92, seven years after her husband.

Her washing machine always had a wringer and she never owned a dryer, hanging the clothes outside to dry. But the clothes off the clothesline always had a fresh clean smell when you put them on. In this way we whiled away the days of our lives. Television was not put on until eight o'clock at night and then off just after the eleven o'clock news. That was the ritual punctuated by commercials when we would rush to the kitchen for tea and cookies or a sandwich before bed. Reading the newspaper was everybody's pastime each day except Sunday when no paper was printed. Discussions about the daily news events peppered our dinnertime conversations. The supper meal was always enjoyable as we got together around a hearty discussion. There was a lot of variety in our weekday meals: pork chops, ham, veal, stews, chicken, fish, ox tails, meat pies, and accompanied by new potatoes, occasionally, fresh out of the ground. Snap peas and beans were a regular as was all the usual fresh summer vegetables of cucumber, tomatoes, onions and mushrooms. Everything was cooked well. There was no pizza, or rarely any fast food at our house. Fish and chips were made at home and always tasted better than from the store. Desserts were at every meal and my grandmother made many of these. She loved to make bread pudding, custard, custard pies, and rice pudding. Today, these never taste the same as I remember them.

When I was twelve years old we went out the back to plant a hawthorn tree about ten or fifteen feet from the lake off to the west side. I dug the hole for planting and hit some object

DAVID WOODWARD

beneath he soil with a clunk of steel agains steel or iron. On persevering further, I managed to drag out of the ground from about two feet depth, a round rusty iron object. It looked like a cannon ball and we all laughed saying something about the War of 1812 and the Battle of the Burlington Races of which we were well aware being devoted history buffs. We went about our business and left it outside in the garden for a very long time. We called it our War of 1812 cannonball, showing to visitors whenever we were out with them in the garden. Over time everyone just forgot about it. Then I did some research years later in my life and I realized it really was what we first thought it was. I must tell the story.

The cannonball I found on our lakeshore property in 1954. I believe it to be from the Battle of the Burlington Races in September, 1813.

On September 28, 1813, a fleet of American warships headed out from Youngstown, New York in the Niagara River towards Toronto. They crossed the lake heading for York, now called Toronto. It seemed Commodore Chauncey of the United States Navy decided to make a name for himself by taking control of Lake Ontario from the British in their quest to invade the northern colony of British North America. War had been going on for more than a year. The British fleet on Lake Erie had been captured by American Admiral Perry and now the Americans controlled that waterway. This prevented

Britain from protecting the western part of Upper Canada. Thus that area was burned out and mostly destroyed by William Henry Harrison and other American military people. Now the British held only the Niagara peninsula area with troops headquartered on Burlington Heights at the Hamilton Cemetery and Dundurn Castle area. If the Americans could capture this area and take control of Lake Ontario, Britain would not have a transport route left to arm troops or provide provisions for survival. Quebec and the rest of the colonies east would be the next target.

At about 10:40 that morning, British Commodore Yeo left his mooring at York with a small fleet to meet the oncoming Americans. On that day, gale force winds roughed up the lake surface making it difficult to maneuver the ships of both navies. They approached one another and circled, firing cannon shot at the opposing side. The Americans fired back. They had a 100 gun ship called *The Pike* and several other warships towing militia. This ship had been named after US General Pike killed in York several months earlier by the explosion of the armoury in Fort York. A cannonball shattered nearby and shrapnel hit his head.

As the ships of each side tried to get the advantage, they sailed further down the lake until, off Bronte, the real battle commenced. People on shore at the time thought there was a regatta going on, because of the odd blast and ships seemingly going past one another to circle the enemy. In due time, The British flag ship, *The Wolfe,* had its mast badly shot to shreds, but they made it safely to anchorage just off the Burlington Beach area where the sandbar protected Burlington Bay. Using a strategy developed by Nelson off the coast of Egypt Yeo and his men had their ships form an arc to prevent being surrounded. The strategy that worked for them to save the day was called the "springs on the cable" maneuver. This battle has never been given its real place in the history of the War of 1812. This was because at the later Battle of Plattsburg, the Wolfe was captured and the ship's log was sent to the Library Congress in Washington, D.C. As a result historians could not know what really took place that day. Chauncey, the American got a chance to write his memoirs where Yeo did not due to an early death after illness. Hence the true story of this battle was never told. Robert J.Williamson[6] claims that the Burlington

DAVID WOODWARD

Races battle was bloody and the real saver of Canada from being taken by US forces. In 2013 on September 28, the exact day of the battle 200 years later, a brief ceremony was held unveiling a new historic plaque in Spencer Smith Park. It was later permanently placed near the water overlooking the site where the British fleet held the day — near where the Brant Inn once stood. For the full story of they battle, see the book <u>Lords of the Lake</u> by Malcomson.[7].

The plaque erected in Spencer Smith Park near the location of the British ships off Burlington Beach in September, 1813

I took my grandson to this dedication event in Spencer Smith Park and the man kneeling in the picture below is an historian and author, CDR Robert James Williamson, CD. I told him about my cannonball and where it was found. He led me to his car and said there was a copy of the Wolfe's ship's log in his trunk and he would see what could be found about the aftermath of the battle. Soon he unrolled the scroll-like paper document and found an entry about the aftermath of battle on that day in 1813. It appears that the ships sailed from their battle-ready anchorage near the sandbar to about 6 miles up the lake. They pulled into a small bay going ashore *"with two gunboats and cannon"*. From the shore they protected the damaged fleet while the masts were repaired for about three-days. There is a small bay off the Burloak Park of today. It has a point that juts out where the Suncor pier is located. In

1954, I found the cannonball which I believe was left there by the party that went ashore for protection of the ships. The cannonball was probably not shot there in battle but merely dropped by the party onshore with the cannon. Williamson told me that that statement from the ship's log is probably the closest proof I would ever get that my cannonball was from that significant battle. I have the artifact to this day as a treasure on my mantle.

Robert Williamson kneels before the new plaque commemorating the Battle of the Burlington Races in Spencer Smith Park, October 28, 2013.

DAVID WOODWARD

6

The Barneses and The Lucketts

In May of 1950, Charles Luckett and his wife Gladys purchased a piece of land next to my grandparents. They were the second owners of this tract of land. It was Lot 1, Concession 4, 71 feet frontage on Lakeshore Highway to the waters edge with riparian rights. Riparian rights, in common law, allowed those who owned land adjacent or bordering on a waterway to use the water for various purposes (i.e. swimming, fishing, and boating and they could put a dock or pier there). If the water level lowered and more land was available, land was deemed to be part of the original deed. If erosion took place, then the land left was whatever remained. Taxes never changed because land had been lost in this way. All lots in this section had riparian rights attached to the land deeds.

The prior owners, James Henry Barnes and his wife, Lily, bought this land to settle in retirement like my grandparents. It was September 1945. Mr Barnes was a minister of some protestant affiliation, I believe. He fenced in the lot on the west and Lakeshore Road sides and planted a number of daffodils but never did any other improvements. Finally, the property was sold to the Lucketts in 1950. I guess he changed his mind.

The Lucketts had a son, James Theodore Luckett whose wife was called Phyllis Roberta, maiden name, Marriott. Phyllis's father and mother were also involved in the use of the property from time to time. Her brother owned a small cabin cruiser and would come ashore there and pick me up at my grandfather's dock for a ride on the lake. He only did that twice. In any case these two families had grandiose ideas about what they were going to do. First the parents said they would build a small dwelling to live in while they built a nice house with a circular drive. They would also add a boathouse and have central heating to it from the house, they told us. A year later, they sold the lot and the small house consisting of three small rooms to their son James and his wife. The only improvements to the land made by these owners was the small dwelling, a well with water to the house, and a circular drive for the cars to turn.

Phyllis Luckett and neighbour, David Woodward, about 1950.
Note the jersey cows on the Kolassa farm in the background.

Phyllis and Jim had three children while living there: Dorothy, Randy and Jayme. She had two children later in Bronte on their next Lakeshore property: Connie and Scott. See picture above for Phyllis Luckett who passed away in 2016. Her husband Jim died in 1999. The family Chow is in the photo also. Note the farm land on the north side of Lakeshore. Cows can be seen by the fence.

Jim Luckett was a salesman for the West Manufacturing Company. I recall he had one short arm but nevertheless was a naval veteran of WWII. He once owned a Henry J Kaiser automobile, a Studebaker car, and later, a Ford Edsel, all interesting cars. They were nice and friendly neighbours. One night I recall fondly, they had a corn roast with barbecue in their back yard. It went on till all hours of the morning and I was dragged away to bed. Guests swam from their beach seen in an earlier picture The music and excitement was a rarity to us in those days; therefore it stands out in my mind. In November, 1954, suddenly, the Lucketts sold the property and moved about a mile down Lakeshore to what was then Bronte. They had a small bungalow back from the road in an empty field next door to the Richard Duke family estate by Sheldon Creek. Duke was the owner of Duke Lawn Equipment company located on Plains Road in Burlington. Every summer, he hosted a garden party with large farm equipment pieces for demonstration on his lawns. Today, his business still exists in the Plains Road area of Burlington near Brant Street. As for the Lucketts, I visited them once in their new home when a teenager. I never saw them again until a retirement celebration for my father-in-law, Paul J. McCarthy He retired from the Department of Veterans Affairs in 1990 after 51 years service with the Navy and Department of Veterans Affairs. He had helped veteran of the navy, James Luckett, apply for a pension and the Lucketts were there to thank him.

7

A Canadian Vaudevillian:
Albert W. Jordan

When I first met this fascinating man I was merely twelve years old. His name was Bert Jordan, or more formally, Albert W. Jordan. He became one of my dearest friends when I was growing up on the shore of Lake Ontario. I always called him Mr. Jordan. Always wearing a baseball-style cap, Albert Jordan could be found smoking his pipe contentedly in conversation by our wire fence. He was a slim man about 155 pounds with clear blue eyes and an inquisitive angular face. His spectacles were framed in a tinted plastic and he usually wore a short sleeved golf shirt as he tended to the watering and the weeds. You could tell by Bert's hands that he had used them thoroughly over the course of his seventy plus years when I came to really know him. Those fingers were all gnarly with arthritis swelling the joints. I wondered if this condition was caused by the balancing and pressure absorbed by his fingers during his acrobatic career in vaudeville acts. Perhaps, I conjectured, this was the result of dampness from pulling weeds over the many years in the garden. His pants were made for his occupation — loose and without any form. His shoes were boot-like and well worn.

Bert's attestation papers from the Great War show that he was a conscript called to duty for his country in the final year of that world-changing event, 1918. His address at that time was given as The Majestic Hotel in Detroit, Michigan. His occupation was "actor acrobat". My grandfather didn't really like the fact that he was a conscript and looked down on that because he had been a volunteer in service at the Front for nearly four of those war years. Bert's first and only destination was Vladivostok, Russia. After a very short time he was sent back home as the war had ended. He recounted very little of that episode in his life or perhaps he preferred to forget it. My grandfather, on the other hand, spoke often about the non-violent events of his war-time service and almost never related any of the shelling and constant danger of trench warfare.

In the spring of 1954, the property next door to our house was sold to this single man in semi-retirement. It was 71 feet frontage along Lakeshore Road and 300 feet deep to the water's edge. Born in a village called Tullamore, Ontario, near Malton by today's Pearson International Airport, Bert became the last child of his mother. He told me that she was 53 years old at the time of his birth, difficult though that is, to believe. Nevertheless I recall him imparting this interesting life event as we strolled up Trafalgar Line one summer morning. When he grew up and needed to find work, Bert counted on his extraordinary athletic skills to make him a living. He drifted away from his hometown and country to the United States in New York City where he found work as a small-time player on stage doing balancing acts in Vaudeville.[8]

In the early days of the twentieth century a popular, relatively inexpensive entertainment industry was in full throttle that soon saw countless numbers of followers: vaudeville. This was an entertainment form popular in North America from about 1880 to 1930. In hundreds of theatres throughout Canada and the United States, performers were grouped together or performed singly by singing, dancing, playing musical instruments, telling jokes or performing skits. Jugglers, magicians, and impersonators were often featured. At the advent of the silent screen movies, vaudeville began to decline and was soon eclipsed by the arrival of "talkies" or sound movies. Many of the vaudevillians got their start in silent movies and talkies. Some of these went on to adapt to television later such as Jimmy Durante, Mae West, and Sophie Tucker. Every city of a certain size in North America had its own theatre where live acts would drift in for a day or two and then they would move on to another town.

VAUDEVILLE

Bert was really taken up with performing but he rarely made enough money to keep him fed and clothed. Nevertheless, for Bert, the thrill of performing on the same stage as the greats of showbiz: Jimmy Durante, Eddie Cantor, Al Jolson, and Sophie Tucker kept him following the theatre circuit throughout the United States. Eventually he did have his name on the theatre billboard with those just mentioned. He had performed in 47 of the then 48 states of America. All states, that is, except Colorado. In time, he teamed up with another athletic performer and they kept the audience thrilled with their balancing routine. The act consisted of difficult formations and using one finger to stand on, for example. I remember him showing me two photograph albums of the performances. These were carefully mounted with black photo corners in his black leather albums.

One example of his humour was a story, Bert told about elephants waiting in the wings to go on stage when the baby elephant used his trunk to grab the adult male elephant's penis and he turned it on the trainer as the great beast urinated backstage. Their act was called "Gordon and Jordan", after their two surnames, of course.

Our acquaintance began with over the fence encounters where we talked about his flowers and vegetable garden and about the weather and all sorts of current events. Fiercely proud of his garden, he would always have a Dutch hoe in hand and a nozzleless hose nearby. That was a habit I copied from him, always preferring no harsh spray that a nozzle projects. The dutch hoe is a garden tool for weeding shallow surfaces. I still use one now in my seventies. It is hard to find one of these now.

What kind of garden did Bert Jordan grow? A very well-planned one indeed! Toward the west side of the property, ranged the vegetable garden with rows of pansies growing, west to east. On the east side next to my grandmother's tall trees he planted shrubs and perennials with a beautiful long rectangular mixed bed of annuals and other perennials. Most noticeable were the pansies and violas which were grown from seed in his cold frame. This was located at the back of a small work shed just before the vegetable garden. Beside the autumn-sown pansy plants, Jordan set up wire frames for sweet peas to climb and perfume the summer garden with the sweetest aromas imaginable.

Further down were a range of Big Boy tomato plants and some Beefsteak varieties. Hills for cucumbers came next, and kohlrabi, Swiss chard, and Jerusalem artichokes. I had never eaten broccoli until I tasted one from Bert's garden. Lastly, closest to the lake, reaching for the sky by mid-summer, cornstalks vied for the bright warm sunlight. Framing the centre-placed lawn on two sides was a golden privet hedge. Near the house, some of my favourite plants grew brightly nodding in the summer breeze. Canterbury bells, delphiniums, nicotiana, evening primrose, and a dozen hybrid-T or multiflora rose varieties. Overhead, a colony of purple martins found their home in an apartment-like structure painted white. It rested on a high pole which was hinged at the bottom, for accessibility to clean. Purple martins are a swallow-like bird that spends early summer skimming and swooping over the lake surface ingesting flying insects, midges, and mosquitoes. They are particularly active at dawn and in early evening. Other bank swallows lived in tunnelled burrows in the lake bank. Here, sand stretched down about two to three feet from the top of the bank. Below this to the lakebed for about thirteen feet were layers of red shale. All in all, the bank was about twenty feet high. Together, these winged creatures made a joyous racket but never one that you couldn't tune out. The rest of the cliff along mighty Lake Ontario, consisted of layered Queenston red shale, (a product of the previous Lake Iroquois that formed the shoreline eons before.).

DAVID WOODWARD

Rear view of the Jordan house from the lake edge

View from Bert's house to the lake

Throughout his garden, Mr. Jordan wove a tapestry of shrubs such as spirea, mock orange, euonymus, forsythia, pussy willow, and English boxwood. These were interspaced with peonies, yucca, gas plant, aquilegia, and so many others. That's how I learned my plant names, from Bert Jordan. All in all, the result was a beautiful tapestry of colour and texture that delighted the eye. One wonderful skill he taught me was how to take a chrysanthemum cutting and pinch it off from the mother plant and stick it in beach sand in a cold frame. There, to watch it grow. As it achieved about 6 inches, buds would form all at the top of each stem. It was easy for these to take root and I enjoyed watching the cuttings increase in size. Jordan would pinch off all flower buds but one. Every day he would repeat this procedure. In the end the mums grew to about 24 inches or more tall until one bud was left to fatten at the apex. This bud opened to reveal a gigantic six inch chrysanthemum flower to the joy of all onlookers. I was ecstatic to be able to do that in my grandparents' garden.

From him I learned so much about gardening little knowing that it would mean a wonderful third career in later life. I learned how to trim a hedge by hand. The importance of pruning down the mock oranges and quinces. Then, of course, I was shown how to prune a fruit tree. Planting pansies from seed usually took months to come to full bloom. We would sow the seed in a cold frame and when the plants were miniature about an inch in diameter we planted them in rows in the greater garden to grow to full size. These beauties with their little faces came in all colours and could be differentiated from their viola cousins by the fact that the latter had no real facial features and were mostly yellow, maroon, or blue. Each April, Mr. Jordan would give me about a dozen plants to take home to Toronto each spring for my family's home garden.

I was fortunate to observe how to vertically string up wire for growing sweet peas and string beans. Beside the sweet peas along the front edge were mound-like boxwoods that lasted forever. They were still there until the Region of Halton pulled them out. I wonder what the new park owners, Halton Region, will do with the remaining species and other trees and shrubs that I remember so well. Will there be any landmark treasures left from my youth as they go about making this a place for everyone? We will have to wait and see.

What a joy it was for me as a city youngster most of the time to behold for the first time a home grown *cypripedium* or lady's slipper with its delicate tress-like slipper ties and the beautiful ballooning form of the moccasin! Then the gas plants which on dewy mornings would flare up when approached with a match or lighter. Their fragrance was like an orangerie full of citrus. A glorious aroma was exuded from the multi-coloured sweet pea which he often presented as a hand bouquet to take to my grandmother's table.

I would water my grandparents's garden as he was spraying his and then we would talk away the early evening by the fence while Jordan smoked his aromatic pipe. In these conversations I learned that he lived in New York City for many years following vaudeville's demise. There he studied horticulture and the art and science of gardening at the New York Botanic Garden. Now a bachelor, Mr. Jordan spoke fleetingly of his earlier marriage saying it broke down because he and his wife had different time clocks in their make-up. He was an early riser and his spouse, the opposite. That's all he ever said of her. I learned via *Ancestry.com* that his wife was born in Manchester England and had been widowed before her marriage to him.

To continue this story, the land next to my grandparents' house had a small 3 room shack on it when it was bought by Bert Jordan in 1954. It must have been no more than six or seven hundred square feet. The previous owners were a young couple with three children and they were always going to build a bigger house but never realized their dream. They sold the property to him and moved to a bigger bungalow next to the Duke Lawn Estate west of the Bronte Village on the same Lakeshore Road.

In May 1954, my grandfather had some surgery at East General Hospital in Toronto and he and Martha stayed in our house there for the recovery period. To get the place ready for their return home, I took the bus from Toronto with my grandmother to cut the grass. I was twelve years old. Having a push mower only, I managed to get the grass cut but we did get the surprise of a new neighbour next door — Mr. Jordan— a pipe-smoking baseball-capped senior who appeared later in his back garden. We noticed he had graded his land and planted flower beds, and vegetables. He had improved the place without doubt. It was nice to know that our new neighbour was a professional gardener.

I was excited. The following week my grandparents rented a taxi to take them both home with a dog, a budgie in a cage their clothing and some food. The fare cost only $50 at the time. They had a 1940 Oldsmobile in the garage but my granddad was not willing to drive it after recent surgery. He was never a reckless man.

About 1958 Albert had a new house built for him to replace

the small abode he called home. Jordan told the builder that he had only $5000 and to "build whatever that amount could purchase." It was a simple house with very small kitchenette, a nook by the south window for his table, and a living room. The hallway connected to the bathroom and 3 small bedrooms at the west end of the house. Two of these were unfinished and just insulated because there was no money to complete them. He slept in the room finished nearest to the rest of the house. It was warm and comfortable and suited Bert for his needs. Sparsely furnished with a bookcase, couch, comfortable easy chair, and a few decorations, the room was cosy enough. A large painting of the sea hung on the west wall. Outside there were some built-in planters and a slight overhang above the entrance doors. No eavestroughs were installed.

Over the years, I became very friendly with Bert Jordan. After dinner when I arrived from Toronto for the weekend, I paid him a Friday night visit at this home. We talked about everything: movies, literature, show-biz personalities he knew, and incidents of our lives as they played out. We discussed the habits of flowers, trees, plants, and the same of birds many of which he could imitate exactly as they sang in pitch and tone. On our walks along the lakeshore and up the town line, (Trafalgar Line, now Burloak Drive), he would pick up the call of a meadowlark, a chickadee, grackle, or raucous blue jay with it's other familiar pump-handle sound. Sometimes it was a wren, a robin, or oriole. He could imitate many of them. Of course then I learned about the two estates where he performed part time gardening duties. These were located in the Port Nelson area of Roseland, Burlington on the lake side. First there was the home of Mrs. Victor Vallance called Lakehurst Villa. What a beautiful garden she had behind the grand stone boulder wall along the highway! Garden parties galore were held there to raise money for the hospital Volunteer Auxiliary of which Mrs. Vallance was president for a while. These were always recorded in the social news of the Burlington Gazette. Preparing for these events was a painstaking affair lasting weeks to get the gardens to their full glory.

Another Jordan employer was the wheel-chair bound Mr. Quigley. He lived next door to the Vallances, in a white wooden board house with black shutters and an attached observatory west of Lakehurst Villa. The gentleman always had a nurse in attendance. I know nothing more about him. His house looks very run down now and will likely be demolished for a grand estate house so common to be built there by the time this book goes to press.

To get to these properties for his day's work, Jordan used the Gray Coach Bus which travelled the Hamilton to Toronto route every hour on the hour. This was the same bus I took home to Toronto Sunday nights. Each way took about 75 minutes with all the stops. It was the same transportation my grandmother used from 1946 to 1961 five days a week as she traveled to work downtown in the main Eaton store, now the Eaton Centre site.

On Friday evenings, or sometimes on Saturday, I would sally forth to an evening of chat about literature with Bert Jordan. There were books to discuss, plots, and characters who were forever ingrained in our minds on the first read. I was introduced to Somerset Maugham, novelist who authored <u>The Razor's Edge</u> and <u>Of Human Bondage</u>. We both liked Dickens, Stephen Leacock, and Mark Twain. I was fond of reading the great philosophers like Socrates and Aristotle. Poetry also figured in what we talked to each other about over the course of an evening. As a student in Toronto's Riverdale Collegiate Institute, my English class contained many of the metaphysical and romantic poets for study. I liked to talk to him about their works as well.

Fred and Bert enjoy a conversation by the fence near
the lake. Both were pipe smokers then.

Then it was time for a cup of tea or coffee and a cookie or two. Then I would be off home next door with enough fodder for pleasant dreams that night. Red Rose tea was the drink he liked and my family, being English, were always drinking tea no matter what time of day or night. The tea box always contained a ceramic miniature bird. I asked Bert to save these for me and I had the whole collection thanks to him.

One particular fond memory I had of this dear friend was the New Year's Day he asked me to come to have an afternoon special dinner of roast duck. I had never eaten duck before and he really was a good cook. I noted that duck had a stronger taste than chicken and it seemed much greasier but it was delicious and made good gravy for the mashed potatoes and green beans. Parsnips and turnip rounded out this special meal to be followed by a home-made coffee cake. We whiled away the afternoon playing pinochle, (pronounced pea-knuckle) using two decks of cards having only 48-cards. It consists of: A (highest),10, K, Q, J, 9, (lowest) in each of the four suits, with two of each card. Less frequently, a 64-card Pinochle pack is used, which includes 8s and 7s as well. The lake provided the backdrop to our game at the table. I lost and have never been good at cards in any case. I truly felt privileged to be invited to share his table on such a special day. It was one of my first real social dinner outings away from my family and I was about seventeen.

The only existent photo of Albert W. Jordan in my possession is reproduced above. He was camera-shy and I sneaked it as he was talking to my grandfather at the fence in 1957 or 58.

A niece of Bert Jordan lived about 500 yards west of him on Lakeshore Road in a yellow bungalow. Her neighbour was a doctor, whose name was Dorothy Mann. I never met nor ever saw her but she lived on the site of today's Burlington Place Retirement Home. His niece was Agnes, married to a man named Jack Barton. Agnes was a middle-aged lady who owned a gift shop boutique on New Street called Agnes Barton: Gifts of Distinction. It was located on the south west side of New at Guelph Line. After his wife died of cancer, Jack Barton became an Anglican minister and I believe he moved to Nova Scotia.

Sadly one fateful morning in 1962, Bert went on a stroll to collect mushrooms and asparagus up Burloak Drive as it was then called. He often did this. Having acquired a small basket of these vegetables for dinner, the old fellow started back across Lakeshore just past the Pig and Whistle Inn. He did not make it across safely. Some young driver heading west in a hurry was impatient and zipped around a slow-moving car only to come in contact with the pedestrian. The good thing was she only grazed him and he sustained injuries to his head and arm. I remember visiting Bert the next weekend at the Joseph Brant Hospital in my University of Toronto, Trinity College blazer. His head had a cut and his arm sported a gash but it was not life-threatening and I felt greatly relieved.

From that event, Mr. Jordan never really recovered completely and he was found several times to be unable to control a tendency to walk backward, unable to stop. He would fall into his garden beds. We thought he might fall over the bank into the lake as we witnessed the backward locomotion several times, powerless to do anything about it. And so it came to pass that Agnes, his niece, decided to take him into her newly purchased house at the corner of Britannia Road and Guelph Line. It was the old United Church manse at Lowville at the corner of Britannia Road. What a fine house with ten foot ceilings it was!

Bert was always independent and self-sufficient. However, I could see that this new life of dependency was killing him but could do nothing to change things for him. I decided to ride my bike to see him in Lowville one summer day. The ride was a hot one and it seemed to go on forever through the back roads of Halton County on the way to the location of his new home. Farms appeared to me as soon as I crossed over the Queen Elizabeth Way on Appleby Line. The first farm on the right going north belonged to Gordie Tapp of TV's "Hee-Haw" fame. The others all the way up to Britannia Road consisted of corn fields mostly and the sun beat down on them without mercy. I took no water and of course had no helmet in those days as was the norm. Nevertheless, I arrived safely in about an hour at the manse. At his new home, Bert was not really happy. He became very forgetful due to his head injury. It seemed like the onset of what today would be like an Alzheimer's condition. I was astounded to see the change in him and very sad to see what had become of this kindly gentleman, my old friend.

He had sold his house to a family of three who lived near

Agnes Barton's Lakeshore house. They had known Jordan from his previous home in Oakville near Dean Avenue. In the next chapter I describe these new neighbours of ours — the Landsboroughs.

Soon I was asked by Agnes Barton to be a pallbearer at Mr. Jordan's funeral. It was a very sad day for me. He has a flat marker in St. Jude's Cemetery in Oakville. For his memory, Agnes gave me his aquamarine birthstone gold ring but I would rather have had his vaudeville picture albums. I could kick myself now for not asking for them then. They were probably discarded by the family anyway as photo albums are often meaningful only to a minority of family members. Bert Jordan gave me many memories to cherish and most of all he encouraged my love of gardening which I turned into a third career that lasted 13 years in my later life after teaching. That opportunity was provided me by Tim Hortons at the corporate Head Office in Oakville and provided a whole campus of corporate property for me to realize my dream job. I continue to do a few properties in town to this day. In fact, I have taken on a job on a 4 1/2 acre estate on the lake in Oakville as well as gardener for a condo complex in downtown Burlington. Another dream from my early days! I have Albert W. Jordan to thank for this legacy he left me.

8
The Landsboroughs:
Mother, Father, Daughter

Margaret Landsborough and her mother, Edith when I first knew
them. Behind is the home Hugh himself built further west on
Lakeshore Road. Two rows of townhouses stand there today

Our last neighbours next door to the west after the Lucketts and Bert Jordan were the Landsboroughs. They moved into Jordan's house in the summer of 1963 as Bert Jordan had to sell it after the accident which left him debilitated. They moved in from just about three hundred yards west along the Lakeshore. A new apartment building was going up next to their home and Edith, the mother, was having none of living next to that. That was in spite the fact that they had only just lived in their new house built by Hugh, the father, for a few years. Margaret and her mother are pictured above in 1957 at the home that Hugh built. If you want to see the house now, it was moved to Maple Avenue on the east side about halfway between Lakeshore Road and the Mapleview Mall. The colour is now grey. One day, Margaret visited Bert Jordan the neighbour next door to us and she saw me in the garden. She asked me if I would come to her home and take some pictures there. I believe the year was 1957 and I used my Kodak Brownie camera to take the photos above.

The Landsborough property was over 300 feet deep and contained an older home at the back on the very shore of the lake. This is the home they bought when they moved to Burlington from Oakville. It might have been the former home of the Crowells. Bert Jordan had been a neighbour of the Landsboroughs on Dean Avenue in Oakville. I do not know who moved to this new location in Burlington first, the Landsboroughs or Mr. Jordan. Today, Margaret cannot recall the answer to that question.

When I first got to know Margaret, it was on one of her visits to Bert Jordan when she exchanged newspapers and vegetable produce that each of them grew in their backyards. This turned out to be a friendly rivalry between them as they tried to outdo one another in gardening. Today, if asked, Margaret still maintains that she was a better gardener than Bert. In her backyard domain, Margaret spent many hours on her knees planting onion sets and gladiola bulbs, tomatoes, and carrots. Sometimes she focused on peas and beans. Always, her garden was extensive with many rows of beautiful specimens. One time, she planted her onions and the dog dug them all up. That is, the dog in the picture, above. Her name was Fanny. Now Fanny took a liking to Bert Jordan. When he visited to share a drink and talk about current events or the gardening highlights each of them experienced that week, Fanny would just sit on the floor in front of Bert Jordan and stare into his face, cocking her head at times from side to side. This made Margaret smile and Bert a little unnerved. Nevertheless they got along and Fanny seemed happy to see callers when they dropped by. Visitors other than Bert appeared very seldom, for the Landsboroughs were a very private family. They kept to themselves and rarely if ever, ventured onto neighbours' premises for a social visit.

Edith, the mother met her husband in the Glasgow area of Scotland. She had been born in Islington, near London but times being tough, she went north and found a job in Glasgow. What job she did there is not known by Margaret as her mother and father talked very little about the old country days. Hugh, the father, apparently had been training to be a cabinet maker but came to Canada and took work in Oakville as a tenant farmer on the Fourth Line. They had a few farm animals and grew vegetables. It was enough to keep the family afloat when a carpentry job was unvailable. Edith assisted with the farm wherever she could. In time they brought out a daughter who had reached the age of sixteen. Her passage document showed that her parents, Hugh and Edith paid the fare and she was going to live with them. Up until then she had been living in London with her grandmother. In 1921 she arrived and was listed on the census form as Molly Landsborough, 16. However, in November 1922, she was married and her marriage certificate listed her name as Mary Edith Landsborough, 19. In one year she had a changed name and gained three extra years. Mary Edith married an English immigrant in Toronto. His name was William George Flowers. They had three children together in Toronto and then in 1936, William left his wife and children and applied for citizenship in New York State. Three years later he received naturalized citizenship and by then was married to a person named Joan. I guess his marriage to Mary didn't work out. Margaret never knew about this sister of hers until I told her, although the documents available online at ancestry.com confirm it is true. In England, Molly, who was really called Mary Edith claimed on her passage document that her closest relative in England was her grandmother, who's married name was Palmer. Edith's maiden name was Palmer. Why is there a mystery in these facts? The ignorance of them by Margaret is unclear but the Landsboroughs were as I said. a private family and they didn't discuss their earlier life much at home it seems. Up until the last few years, Margaret thought she was an only child

The year Mary Edith got married was 1922. Margaret was born in October, 1921. She was delivered by a midwife who lived on an adjacent farm. Margaret was told that she was named after her mother's favourite sister. She attended elementary school in Oakville and remains unsure of when she left school to work. Her first job was in a grocery store in Oakville. Later she joined an air coil manufacturing company on Wyecroft Road and continued in that employment for over 30 years. In her lunchtimes and break moments, Margaret played cards with "the boys" and she was known as a very productive worker.

Sometime later, Hugh got word that they were looking for qualified cabinet makers and carpenters at the site of the new Brock Hotel in Niagara Falls. He was hired for the job when he proved he had a set of good tools. The family moved to Lundy's Lane in Niagara Falls near the grave site of Laura Secord. In fact her monument was right across the street from their home. On the front near the steps of their home, they found an iron stake in the ground. Local legend spun a story that that was where Laura Secord tied up her cow. To this day, Margaret loves to tell that story. It didn't matter that Laura Secord, the Battle of Beaver Dams heroin of 1812, lived in Queenston in those days. It is an interesting fact that Laura Secord was granted land in Burlington — 200 acres, where the present Paletta Park is located at the corner of Secord Lane and Lakeshore Road. Laura Secord never lived there. This is less than a mile from Burloak Waterfront Park. Again they had a wonderful garden in the backyard and the Niagara mists dropped lots of moisture on whatever was planted.

When I asked her mother about those days she always said that Niagara Falls was not real beauty — it was man-made beauty, hence not the real thing. I guess, having lived in Scotland, she considered natural beauty the only kind to be admired. Still later, the family moved closer to Oakville and Dean Avenue near Kerr Street, above Lakeshore Road. It seems that was when Margaret went to work for a living and helped support the family. She grew up an obedient and hard-working child on the farm and in the garden from her early

DAVID WOODWARD

days. Possessing a bright mind and naturally inquisitive nature, Margaret learned many tasks including the skill of embroidery. She loved to read and always maintained an interest in current events which maintains to this day. Anyone talking to her about recent news would be astounded to realize her depth of awareness of news events and the detail she can recall.

In the fifties and sixties along the lakeshore, many homes had a name sign posted outside on the road. My grandfather called his home Covertside, after a place in Lancashire where he had been born. I have the sign in my back garden shed to this day. Next door to Margaret's first lakeshore home, lived the Tomlinson family. John Tomlinson named his property, Melody Lane and the name was mounted on a white wooden wagon wheel by the driveway entrance. Next door, Margaret's family hung a sign called MYOBB. I asked Margaret what it meant one day and she said, "Mind Your own Blooming Business." So privacy obviously meant a great deal to the family. When the parents had passed on, the sign came down!

Upon purchasing the land and home of Bert Jordan, it needed some renovations to accommodate three people. Therefore, in the autumn of 1963, Hugh arrived one day with a pile of wood for construction. He altered the house by putting in a wood-burning fireplace above which he panelled, in natural knotty pine, the eastern wall. Hugh also added a sitting room with wood stove on the back of that facing the lake. When digging out the basement part of the new addition, they discovered a natural spring pouring water in the corner of what was to be the only cellar area of the house. Thus it was necessary to build the cellar with cement blocks for a storage area. A sump pump he installed to take out the spring water. From the outside they installed a stairway with folding doors that covered them. Finally, though Bert had a shed out back, Hugh felt it necessary add another addition to it in order to store firewood. Margaret proceeded to reinvent the garden in her own style and taking Bert's legacy, she made it her own creation. She set about designing a garden like she had before at the other lakeshore home. She too, made it magnificent with birdbath and lawn chairs to look at, for no one ever sat in them. They added a fence along the lake to keep the dog in.

In 1965, the family decided to purchase the lot next door to the west of them which consisted of a 100 feet frontage. It was bought for $10,000. This was the lot my grandmother wanted to purchase for their home back in 1942 but the owner, a Mrs. Marshall of Detroit, Michigan would only sell lots in order from east to west. In 1942 the only lots for sale were adjacent to the Bolus Lakeshore park site and/or the property adjacent to the Eales property. My grandparents chose the latter. They would have loved to own the empty lot the Landsboroughs bought. It was never built on and over time lost all of a dozen tamarack trees located by the shore as they tumbled through erosion into the lake year by year.

Margaret feeding some geese near her back door.

When I was quite young I remember this lot growing weeds each summer that stood as high as two or three feet- mainly Queen Anne's Lace, goldenrod, timothy grass, mullein, and burdock. The township of Nelson came by once a season in the summer to control allergy-causing pollen. They started a fire when the wind was right so that it blew the flames through the tall grass toward the lake, leaving a scorched earth ready to grow again. There was no necessity then to mow it. The tax bill showed a fee added for this service.

In the year 1969 the lot was sold by the Landsboroughs for nearly the same price as they had paid themselves. It had been an investment.

As time went on, Hugh, a very tall man became frail and

DAVID WOODWARD

had a stroke or some kind of major physical event that left him bedridden. He soon developed dementia. Neither Edith nor Margaret could consider sending their husband and father to a nursing home or retirement home, therefore, they decided to look after him until the end. It was very trying on the two women to look after his feedings and washing and to have to attend a person who didn't even know them anymore. Mrs. Landsborough used to tell me that they washed Hugh, "all 99 per cent!" I guess Hugh did the other one percent but I never asked. They took on this onerous responsibility until Hugh's passing in 1973 with dogged determination and independence while continuing life as normal as they could. Edith lived for ten more years until she broke her hip, developed pneumonia, and died in hospital. Margaret lived on for 31 more years alone in the middle the park until 2014 when declining health forced her to move to a retirement home. She still resides near her former home on the lake.

9

The Sparkle in His Eye Turned to Gold: The Koleffs

Kiro and Beatrice Koleff by their large steel-hulled launch,
the *Kirobea*, built in Bronte at Metro Marine.

There was gold in his eyes and he would seek out his dream
in Canada. This man of the lakeshore was Kiro Koleff, born
in Bulgaria in 1894, the son of a mayor of his town. All over
the Balkans, the Ukraine and Bulgaria, around the time of the
Balkan Wars (1912–1914) signs lured this enterprising young
man to seek the land of gold in the wheat fields of Canada.

However, the gold colour that Kiro sought was not edible

like wheat but shiny, durable, and metal — real gold. To get away from the possibility of an upcoming war, Kiro sailed to Canada aboard the *Potsdam* from Rotterdam to Halifax. His ship arrived December 29, 1913. Kiro found himself in Montreal. He became a chauffeur to a doctor there. Eventually, given his wanderlust, he made his way to the north in Ontario and the Sudbury mines. His driving skills in Montreal earned him a job driving an electric tram underground. Koleff started to save his meagre wages hoping one day to buy a goldmine. He told me that with his first pay he bought a pair of heavy work gloves to protect his blistered hands from the rough wood that goes into shoring up the mine tunnels. He also got roughed up by the railroad ties that he occasionally was directed to help lay. This part of mining was beginning to take the sparkle off his goal.

It was in Sudbury where he met a girl from the Ukraine who was barely sixteen at the time. He asked her father for his blessing for marriage. The old man agreed after being offered a case of whisky. Kiro was a promising husband, strong, tall, and immensely good-looking. He always wore the best of clothes and made an imposing figure. Beatrice, from the Ukraine, herself an immigrant born in 1904, fell madly in love with him and they married in that mining town..

Their very large wedding was the talk of the town due to the number of guests. It was the largest Ukrainian wedding ever to take place in Sudbury until that time. I remember seeing a photo taken following the ceremony with literally hundreds of folk against a drab wooden building so common in mining towns. There were musicians with violins and a cello and everyone was in their Sunday best dress. so many guests were in attendance and they celebrated for four days before going home and back to work. A wedding was one of the only times that work was interrupted for a happy festive occasion. Their love sustained them through the course of their lives and was obvious to all who knew them.

In Sudbury, Kiro started driving a taxi, and before long he had a fleet of taxis. His entrepreneur spirit continued his whole life long in Canada. Over the next few years, he acquired a second taxi company and benefited from the profits it yielded. Beatrice was blessed with a golden voice and was renowned for her singing in the community. Years later, I witnessed her singing the Anniversary Waltz aboard their yacht, the *Kirobea*. Together they bought a hotel called the Thunder Bay in Geraldton. Thunder Bay, as the city is now called, was known as Port Arthur and Fort William then, — two side by side twin cities on the shore of Lake Superior. In the northern country of beautiful lakes carrying beautiful yachts and cabin cruisers, Kiro dreamed of one day owning his own boat. He wanted so much to drift around the lake. But Kiro loved the Ontario northland most of all. With an adventurous, pioneering spirit, Kiro set out to prospect and make mining claims. His passion soon took to prospecting with great enthusiasm. He would venture out with his axe pick in search of rocks bearing a motherlode of some precious metal. In due course, his search was to be fulfilled. He staked a claim in Setting Net Lake area of the Kenora District on land which showed veins of gold, copper, and nickel. The mine sold shares and became somewhat profitable, yielding dividends over many years.

In due course, Kiro and Bea, as they were called by all, had a daughter, Ollie, in Sudbury. She was born in 1922. This couple had to find a way to make a steady living and they built a hotel and then a number of smaller ones for loggers. Bea hired the staff and managed a larger rooming house for log workers, also supervising the kitchen and the care of the rooms. She worked very hard honing her skills at management and organization there.

Some times they would take a trip to Niagara district driving along the lakeshore to buy fresh fruit there and take it home to the north. It was then that they became attracted to Lake Ontario and the Burlington area. The three of them found their way to Burlington to begin the next chapter in their lives. They acquired land on Lakeshore Road in Port Nelson, now downtown Burlington. The couple built a house fronting on the lake opposite Beaver Street where it still stands. This house was a two story white-framed building which set the scene for many warm family gatherings and parties. Indeed, their daughter Ollie was married in the garden there by the lake in 1950.

In the late 40's Kiro and Bea noticed a property that was vacant land several miles east and about a mile and a half west of Bronte. They inquired to see if it was for sale and subsequently bought it. There they built their next home.

Over the next years we gradually came to know and enjoy our new neighbours.

The first residence owned by the Koleffs in Burlington was the one mentioned above. It was built in 1939 and scene of many warm and friendly family gatherings and small parties. In the late forties, it was time to look for a new location to live in and another lake property. As stated above, Bea and Kiro found a piece of land further down the lakeshore beside the private, Lakeshore Park. This land had its own shingle rock beach full of grey, flat sedimentary rocks, and many small and beautiful smooth igneous rocks. There were quartz stones, feldspar, schists, and gneisses, muscovite, mica, and granites. It was fun to spend all day trying to find fossils wading barefoot along the smooth stones. The park on the western boundary of today's Burloak Park was owned by a Greek immigrant Sam Bolus. He later sold it to another immigrant family from Winnipeg, originally from Poland. Macedonian and Orthodox church groups came from Toronto, Hamilton, and other locations for ethnic picnics on Sundays after churches selected that location. More about this can be found in the following chapter.

The lady who owned this strip of land from Bolus's to the Pig and Whistle was Mrs. Edna Marshall from Detroit. Her father, Frank Hay, left her a large number of acres from the Nelson Township Line going west to the park. He had owned both sides of the Toronto Hamilton Highway, and bequeathed it to her. By now she was married to an American who lived in the United States. She visited her old properties and the buyers who bought from her for many years each summer, insisting that new purchases be made next to the previously-sold ones. Therefore, Kiro bought the land beside the existing private park. That left one and only one piece of undeveloped land in the middle of the park next to the Koleffs. It was owned by several different people but never built on.

Kiro's new property had some very special other features. A beautiful huge laurel tree with shiny dark green leaves graced the edge of the beach. A small grove of tamarack trees stood at the edge of the vacant land next door. All these trees were lost by the 80's due to erosion of the shoreline. The lot was gently sloped upwards on both sides to allow access to the beach in some natural geological formation and the shale banks rose

DAVID WOODWARD

on the borders of the property to about twenty feet high. Koleff had a gentle sloping access right to the water. This was the flat-stoned shingle beach we all loved so much.

The Koleff Beach around 1945, before they owned it. Note the flat round rocks suitable for skipping on the water. My mother is left at back and I am the long-haired child of about 3 years. Tamarack trees are top left.

The new owners designed an H-shaped residence of one story. The bedrooms, kitchen, and bathrooms were on the sides and the living room and dining room in the middle cross section. A fine patio of flagstones was placed at the back and a separate garage stood apart at the western side. Originally, there grew a large old willow tree in the middle of the front lawn but the Koleffs had it bulldozed and I remember when I came out for the weekend to discover that I was very upset because I loved every willow tree in the area. They were fun to climb. He was right to cut it down as it really didn't belong in the middle of the front lawn. (They planted a willow later at the back). In addition on the west side were planted ten fruit trees with lilacs and honeysuckles on the east side. It was near the laurel tree where a large storm water pipe emptied onto the beach. In the rush of water, a large hole was formed into which I fell when I was about 5 years old and all by myself. I don't know how I managed to get out from the freezing November water. But I made it home. For me, this plot of land had been free and open for the picnickers at the park next door and for anyone to wander on. There had been no fence until the Koleff's bought there. I considered it my own domain — nearly half the extent of today's Burloak Waterfront Park. The beach was the attraction. In those days kids were allowed to go outside unaccompanied to play. Sometimes they got into situations that were dangerous and had to learn how to avoid these the next time. Experience was a good teacher. I learned a lot by myself as an only child in this way.

Kiro and Bea's H–shaped home as viewed from their beach.

Over time, when I was about 13 or 14 years old. Mr. Koleff appeared at my grandfather's door and asked if I was there. He proposed that I might like to cut his grass once a week and earn a few dollars. I easily accepted the offer. This was the beginning of a relationship that grew over the years into a friendship with the whole family. I cut his lawn for many years.

At the back of his property, in the full sunlight of summer, Kiro had an above ground pool put there for his grandchildren, Carol and Keith Bristow. This was great attraction for them and they seemed to be always there when I cut the grass. Their mother, Ollie Bristow, was the first psychologist hired by the Burlington Board of Education. She also earned a teaching certificate which meant she was remunerated according to the teachers' pay scale. When I took a break with a bottle of Pepsi or Coke, we would talk. I got to enjoy the conversations. It is a nice memory to remember the mirthful laughter of the grandchildren who were about seven or eight years younger than I. Carol and Keith I thoroughly enjoyed when they were playing around the pool. Both were energetic, running and chasing each other or some butterflies and in general being carefree children. Carol was like her brother, always willing to climb a tree or go exploring in the near fields. They were a joy to watch. Sadly Keith was merely fifteen when he suddenly developed leukemia, which, in a few months, claimed the young boy's life. It was a great tragedy for such a happy family. Keith was a blond, handsome lad full of exuberance and play as a young child. I will always remember him with Carol, his sister, at their grandparents' home.

In 1953, always a risk taker, Kiro invested in a block long building on Brant Street at the corner of James, opposite the City Hall. He added a second story at the back. Several restaurants have located in that building in recent times but real estate offices, a dentist and orthodontist, a hairdresser, bicycle repair shop, and Dorothy's School of Dance had all rented premises there. The property owners now are currently in a controversial battle with those who do not want a Brant Street and downtown to be hemmed in with skyscrapers. A sign, "Koleff Building" used to be found on the James Street side of the present building. While under his ownership, during Mayor Lockhart's time, business leaders on Brant Street asked Kiro Koleff's son-in-law, Eric, to run for mayor. He declined.

Ollie's husband Eric Bristow was a land developer of residential areas and commercial real estate in Burlington. One of the areas designed by Eric was Glen Afton Estates near Shoreacres Road and Spruce Avenue. Another residential street he planned with the help of his father-in-law, Kiro Koleff, was the street called Crestwood Court. This was a former estate land purchased by Koleff as an investment It is situated south just off Lakeshore Road near Appleby Line. After a short time in the Canadian Army, the Queen's Own Rifles, Eric enlisted in the RCAF and became a tail gunner in the Lancaster bombers. These flew out of England flying over Germany to weaken and destroy the growing tyranny of Hitler so that he couldn't take over the British Isles as he had done to most of western Europe.

Eric's unit was No. 419 (Moose) Squadron. This squadron was one of the most decorated units of the RCAF during the war. On the Ides of March 1945 in German territory, his plane was shot down. As he bailed out, the fire from the blazing plane burned him badly about his face, hands and body. Nevertheless, he was able to save one of his crew while exiting the burning plane. Since WWII was nearly over, the German soldiers who found him cared for Eric until the British troops arrived to liberate Europe. They sent him to England for treatment. Due to the severe burns he was sent to the remarkable burn unit at the Queen Victoria Hospital where he miraculously came under the care of Dr. Ross Tilley, a Canadian surgeon,[9] and Dr. Sir Archibald McIndoe in East Grinstead, England. McIndoe was a New Zealander. There, under these two fine doctors, he was one of 149 Canadians who underwent innovative reconstructive surgery to treat his significant burns. Over 600 military men were treated in East Grinstead.[10] These airmen called themselves the "Guinea Pigs" and later formed the Guinea Pig Club whose honorary president is Prince Philip. The Canadian president of the same group became Dr. Ross Tilley. As for Eric Bristow and the Guinea Pigs, Eric's daughter, Carol is working with others on an exhibit to be displayed in the Warplane Heritage Museum in Hamilton to be on view sometime in 2018.

I inquired of Ollie's daughter, Carol, how Ollie met the young man who would be her husband. She apparently crossed paths in a hospital with this injured airman and felt very badly about seeing him in this severely weakened state. She left him a note wishing him well, hoping for his speedy recovery. Ollie was that kind of young woman — concerned about others who were less fortunate than herself. Now in 1948, after studying at McMaster University and the University of Toronto, she went to Western University in London, Ontario to pursue a master's degree. It was here, in London, that she started volunteering at the Wellington Hospital. A graduate in psychology, Ollie wanted to help with the returning servicemen who were trying

DAVID WOODWARD

to deal with the effects of "shell shock", now called PTSD. Ollie volunteered to bring some joy and laughter to the patients by taking them to the canteen, playing card games, and generally cheering them up in a social atmosphere.

By chance, one of Eric's close air force buddies was a patient at this hospital and he wrote to Eric that he should come and visit him because these the girls were a sight to behold at Wellington. Eric made a visit to his friend. He was introduced to Ollie through his friend and soon they realized their short acquaintance and the note written in passing the previous year. Eric was smitten and soon began making trips each weekend to see Ollie. In 1950 they were married in Ollie's parents' back yard in Burlington.

Eventually, Eric and Ollie, with their children, moved to a new address on Stratheden Drive in Burlington. Later they moved opposite the Joseph Brant Museum for a time before finally moving to the Lakeshore near where Ollie's parents started out. The couple settled in the Port Nelson area in a waterfront property still in the family. Ollie was the kindest lady whose knowledge of children and psych-social issues affecting their lives was to be her life's work.[11] She assisted countless parents, principals, teachers, and students during her tenure with the Halton Board Education.

In 1968 the Koleffs left their latest Lakeshore beach home, later selling it to the City of Burlington. They moved to an estate with a red brick farmhouse-like residence. There were numerous apple trees on the large estate-sized lot one block west of Appleby Line. Soon I was asked by Mr. Koleff to be the grass cutter there too.

This property was quite large. It was a two-storied brick home with garage surrounded by many maple and fruit trees. Cutting grass around these was quite a chore, especially with fallen apples. Almost immediately Kiro and his wife commenced renovations and remodelling to update the house. They hired others I knew to help spruce up the place. John Kolassa, the farmer who lived across from my grandparents was one of these. He and I tried to put an oil compound on the wooden roof shingles to help preserve them but they were so dry we gave up. The dry shingles soaked up the first multi-gallon can almost immediately. Thus we gave up after only a small patch was done with about 20 gallons. John's wife had been a weekly cleaner of the Koleff's home just across the road at their former place. She continued to clean and maintain the new home on a weekly basis. In the next few years this estate was divided into lots and it became a new street with homes for the more affluent. This is the street designed by Eric. The original house is still there but the brick has been painted white.[12] Burlington doctor Thibideau later purchased the new house next door for his residence.

The original estate house on what is now Crestwood
Court. Another Koleff residence.

The Koleffs vacated this house and returned to to their previous home by the beach again for a time. Then the couple sold that house and property to the City of Burlington. They moved again along the Lakeshore closer to the downtown. Their final move was to locate next to their daughter, Ollie. The house had been sold to them by the retiring Director of Nursing of the Joseph Brant Hospital, Betty Davidson. Since then, granddaughter Carol and family lived there for a while. It was later sold and is currently being built on with a large modern home. Today the family, Carol, her husband Harry, and her children, Christine and Michael live in the house next door. This was her parents' house in which she grew up.

Kiro Koleff passed away in 1985 and Beatrice in 1990. During their lifetime they accomplished a great deal contributing widely to the communities in which they lived. Kiro and Beatrice realized most of their life dreams!

Coincidentally, when I became principal of Lakeshore Public School, in Burlington I was fortunate to have Kiro and Bea's two great-grandchildren in my school, Christina and Michael. But they say nothing is coincidence if you believe Deepak Chopra.[13] Christina followed her mother and grandmother into education and became a teacher at a Burlington high school. Who knows, "coincidentally", she might even teach my own grandchildren as they attend the high school where she teaches. Christina's mother was a teacher of art for a time in the public school system in Burlington. Now Carol spends her time working on commissions as an artist. She has a unique style — meticulously detailed, drawing on a large canvas, a particular treasured object cherished by the client. The medium is pencil and is surrounded with a recurring phrase. The phrase has a particular meaning to the object and client. She was recently acclaimed as an exceptional talent in a recent art exhibition at the Hamilton Art Gallery. She won the Best in Show prize in 2016. and Honourable Mention in a different show in 2017 at the same gallery.

Therefore, in a way, Kiro did find gold in the new world. He made a happy life for himself through his entrepreneurial spirit and hard work which brought him good fortune throughout his life. He left his family a wonderful legacy. In the eyes of his wife, his daughter and his grandchildren, he had struck gold.

10

The Bolus Family

Our neighbours, further west, who owned the seven acre park were Sophia and Sam Bolus. They operated a restaurant and group of cottages with heat and running water. Sam was white-haired and very talkative. He and his wife offered us the use of their well for water which we carried home in a large thermos container. There was no other source of water for us at the time. I remember many times accompanying my grandmother, thermos in a wagon, heading down the shoulder of the road to the well at Bolus's. This well was at the back of the restaurant. I am not sure how he managed to have running water in the cabins which were painted white with small verandahs at each door.

At Bolus's restaurant, one could buy Neilson's ice cream mello-roll cones. These were cylindrical-shaped ice cream that were rolled with paper that was easily pulled off when the proprietor fitted the cylinder of ice cream into the biscuit cone. The cost was five cents. I remember it going up one day to six cents and how indignant I was at the raise in price. Mr. Bolus, as I called him was always obliging, however and I soon forgave hime for the extra cost.

Postcard in the collection of the Oakville Historical
Society's archive. It is available to anyone with no
permission required. The Bolus family restaurant.

His restaurant served many fine meals but he was famous
for chicken dinners. At the west side, a screened in porch was
used for summer customers. At the front he sold some vegetables at a stand and had a gas bar for cars with two pumps.
All in all it was nice to have a place in the community that
served as a kind of confectionery as well as a restaurant. It was
he who started the tradition of Greek picnics each summer
Sunday for all the Orthodox Greek immigrant churches from
Toronto to Stoney Creek. On Sundays one could always hear
the small band which included drums, a clarinet, a violin, an
accordion or zither-like instrument, and sometimes a trumpet.
Some signs were in English, some in Greek or cyrillic script.

Sam and his wife Sophia lived in Hamilton prior to leasing
the Nelson township land. Then they arranged to buy it and
built the restaurant. They had a son George. who was born in
Stoney Creek area but both parents were from Greece. After
selling the cabins and restaurant they opened a new eating
establishment at Plains Road and number 6 Highway called the
Shamrock Inn. George had two sons, Steve, a wrestler, and Dan,
owner of the Top Hat Motel on Lakeshore about 200 yards from
Sam's old place. That motel and park was smaller than Sam's
but it stood where the Diplomat condominium is now.

Over the years, George frequently tended to a derelict plot
of land in Aldershot at the corner of Plains and Francis Roads.
He beautified it and groomed it every spring. Today there is a
parkette there in his name- Bolus Parkette.

DAVID WOODWARD

11
Joseph and Bertha Kowal
and their Family

LAKESHORE PARK MOTEL AND RESTAURANT

Joe and Bertha Kowal leave Winnipeg bound for
their new life in Nelson Township, 1949.

Sophie, Adeline, Carrie, Olga, Frank, Stanley, Jeanett, and
Darlene were the children of the Kowal family of Lakeshore
Park. Their parents, Joseph and Bertha moved from Tuelon,
Manitoba to purchase a business that all the family would be

able to help manage. It wouldn't be a farm. Joe didn't want his children all growing up to be farmers. He was born in Poland. Times were tough after the war years there and he decided to go to America — more particularly, the United States. However, as chance would have it, one night he consulted a fortune teller about his life and the fortune teller told him not to go there but to Canada and he would prosper and have eight children. So he emigrated to Canada and met a local girl on a farm about 30 miles outside of Winnipeg, called Oak Bank. Bertha, was going with another suitor but Joe won her heart and she found that he had some sense of making money when he bought a small farm and sold it at a profit. Sometime later, an acquaintance he met knew of a place he might like to purchase on Lake Ontario near Burlington. It had seven acres and a restaurant business with cabins equipped with running water. Seeking opportunity for a better life for his family, Joe convinced Bertha that it would be better to move to Ontario with their large family in tow. Sam Bolus sold them his business and land in 1949. This was the park, restaurant, and cabins that Sam Bolus built a number of years earlier. On the property there were two wells. The Kowals settled into their new life on Lakeshore Road.

My mother, Aleda, with me in about 1944 sitting in Lakeshore Park. The Eales residence is in the background.

A cheerful, happy group of girls of various ages from about three to teenage years greeted the passerby who might stop for a sandwich or hot dog and french fries. Sometimes it was coffee or a pop as they went about their daily routines along

Lakeshore Road. For the neighbours of the area, there was always a small local store where they could purchase an ice cream or cigarettes, or a bag of chips. Bertha and the elder children mostly managed the counter sales. and made the restaurant meals. Joe looked after the business, keeping supplies up, repairing broken items in the restaurant and the cabins which were rented to tourists and travellers at a modest price.

In the spring Bertha kept gloxinias on all the window ledges to make the room cheerful for guests in between her never-ending chores. In between selling at the counter, cleaning, washing and looking after the needs of her growing family, she also helped with the accounts.

After a few years, it became apparent that cabins were being outdated and they must move ahead and think about a motel to replace the cabins. In time, 18 rooms were built where most cabins had formerly rested and they formed an L-shaped structure. In front on the highway, the old restaurant was razed after a fire and in its place a brand new brick building with two stories filled the void. This was the new home for a growing family. As I was growing up, I would often walk down to the restaurant-store and buy an ice cream cone as I had done before. I became friends mostly with the youngest daughter, Jeannett. She was several years younger than I and we often played together in the park or out at the back. In a few years, Bertha would give birth to her last child, Darlene.

Joe, the father, was not an easy man to know and I don't remember having him sit down and relax very often. He always seemed anxious and had to continue one task after the other. Joe and I rarely got to talk on a personal basis. He must have been a strong man to carry on the hours of work that he did. There were two gas pumps at the roadside and in those days it was nothing for a passerby to ring the doorbell at three o'clock in the morning for gas. No one pumped their own gas in those days! Sometimes they would even follow with a request of a bite to eat. However, Joe was very kind-hearted and rarely turned down a request for something to eat when some labourer walking up the road appeared asking for a free meal.

Bertha Kowal, the matriarch of the family, was a wonderful mother, strong, tender, and loving to her husband and children. Her smile was infectious. She never complained about the difficult life she lived. Never did I hear her criticize anyone. Often she visited my grandparents for tea in the afternoon and they would chat about the children and happy times. After Joe died in 1971, Bertha married again to Carmen Anderson, a Canadian veteran of WWII, having served in Holland with his brother. Carmen liked to wear a bola tie usually. He became a regular visitor with Bertha to our house too. She lived to the ripe age of 99 and lost her sight in the last few years but she had a sharp mind to the end. I remember how welcome she made her old friends feel when they visited her during her last years with two daughters in Burlington.

Sophie, the eldest was not known much to me as she was an adult when I first became regular visitor. Soon she was married to truck driver, John Chopick. They lived in a small cottage on the property near the motel but facing the highway. It was there that my future wife was to live for summer in 1958 unimagined by me at the time, of course. The Chopicks had 3 children, Jerry, Susie, and John. Full of fun, they played mostly around the back of the restaurant and in the park. I do not know when they moved away and the cottage became a rental. In an aside, I should mention that my wife's family resided in the Chopick house during the summer of 1958. The father was a naval warrant officer in the Royal Canadian Navy and was stationed in Hamilton at the HMCS Star base for summer training. Our relationship grew from that summer but I didn't see her again until we were both at university in Toronto five years later.

Adeline, next in line, was a very sweet young lady, always willing to have a chat and ask about my family. Adeline always had a philosophical side that appeared as wisdom as she offered to listen and empathize with whomever confided in her. She appeared to do much of the work in the cooking and preparation area of the kitchen behind the seating area. The tables in the large windowed restaurant were made of arborite, typical of the fifties in diners and eateries such as this. Adeline served her guests with a cheerfulness that endeared her to cus-tomers. She was the second daughter to marry. I remember, as her wedding approached, my grandfather received a knock on the back door of his home when I happened to be there. It was Joe Kowal. He told my grandfather, "Adeline is getting married on Saturday to Steve, a Stelco employee, and I must be at the wedding with the whole family. Can you help us out while we are away because I cannot really close the restaurant or motel? I need someone to stay in charge for 5 or 6 hours. I would really like you and the Mrs. to do it."

The answer was, "Yes, he'd be glad to help out with Martha. Of course, I went along too. We managed the counter business selling cigarettes and confection items to about three dozen people from late afternoon until about 2:00 am when the wedding reception broke up and everyone arrived back. My grandfather did double duty, taking prospective overnight guests to see the motel rooms with a flashlight. We did a good job and the family was pleased. However, we, their good neighbours, were glad not to have to be responsible for this kind of business on a regular basis. When the request was made again for another daughter, my grandfather regretfully declined saying he was getting too old. My grandparents were getting on in age, after all. Steve and Adeline lived there for a while in the restaurant before they built a house in Hamilton. Later they eventually bought a home in Elizabeth Gardens where they still reside. They had two sons and a daughter, Edward, David, and Sandra.

Carrie, the third daughter presented herself at the counter many times greeting guests and customers usually with a flower in her upswept hair. She seemed the most romantic of the sisters and always had a happy smile. What a gentle disposition Carrie had! She lives in Burlington today and is still the same warm person. In time she married a young man named Fred Pentland and they had a daughter, Sheila. Unfortunately, tragedy led to a fatal car accident when Fred was on a fishing/ hunting trip up north. Carrie continued to live at her mother's home in Burlington where she still resides..

Olga was the most serious of the siblings as I remember anyway. Surprisingly, she had a wicked sense of humour and would often tease. She also worked hard in food preparation, cooking, and cleaning as well as preparing linen for the motel. Unfortunately, Olga did not have a long adult life, passing on too early.

Then there was Frank, the elder son. He was in the early teens when I first knew him. I never knew him well for he was always busy attending to the urgencies of each day. He also had a job at Long Manufacturing in Oakville, where he worked with the finance area of the company. Frank soon took an interest in the local union as a leader. He was the one Joe and the family relied on to solve family and business problems the most. He was the rock on whom his parents and sisters often depended for advice.

Stanley was older than I but the one I got to know the best of the two boys. He did much of the heavy outdoor work — especially in the park and in fixing machinery, cutting the seven acres of parkland grass, etc. Lakeshore Park, as it was called, was another part of the business and very lucrative on weekends. Scattered over the seven acres behind the motel and stretching east to the boundary, the property contained numerous picnic tables. These were repaired by Frank and Stanley and Joe at the beginning of each summer season. They made them desirable for visitors seeking a picnic and placed them in various areas. Some were place in sunny locations and near the lake, others under willow trees for shade. When visitors arrived, Stanley would collect 50 cents per carload from the gate entrance off the highway. Sometimes he would let me collect for him but it was rare. At night a wire barrier was put up at the entrance to stop people parking in the dark. The Kowals operated a gas station with two tanks on the site for many years. Several family members pumped the gas day and night. Stan never really had a childhood, I believe, for he was always busy doing chores. He was a hard worker. Later he became a roofer and with his son still runs a successful roofing business in Burlington.

Note all the elm trees along Lakeshore Road which, later, were felled due to Dutch elm disease. Kolassa's 86 acre farm is across the road.

DAVID WOODWARD

Jeannett and Darlene were the youngest girls of the Kowal family. They seemed always happy at play and involved in all the adults' family business as well. In this family everyone had a job to do and sometimes three or four. When I went to visit I usually sat out at the back or in the back family room playing cards or just talking to one or the other as they would have to get up to attend the store frequently. Jeannett became a successful business woman in real estate and now designs kitchens. She, too, was full of fun and keen to help anyone she met. Darlene, very outgoing and entrepreneurial, once wrote a book about shopping for bargains in the United States along the Niagara Falls-Buffalo border region. She was a good student and applied her skills as a professional dental hygienist for a time. Later she bought, renovated, and sold houses. Always a go-getter, Darlene became an owner of four McDonald franchises in Ft. Myers, Florida, where she lives now. She has 2 children, Allison and Michael.

LAKESHORE PARK IN THE 60'S AND GREEK SUNDAY PICNICS

Weekends, Sundays in particular, were busy days during the summer months at Lakeshore Park. As mentioned previously, Greek or Macedonian churches from Hamilton and Toronto used to reserve the park for their annual picnics. Buses as well as cars brought the congregations for the day. Always they brought with them a band to play the traditional old country dance music. I learned to dance in a circle and on occasion, would join in. Most interesting to me was the serious emotion that the men put into their dancing. They would brace each others' shoulders arm to arm in a semi-circle bending deeply almost to the ground in response to the bouzouki and clarinet music. Handkerchieves waved from the lead man's fingers as he went forward, sideways, and then back. It was poetry and art to watch this very emotional expression of dance. I always went there Sundays to watch and sometimes take part. Once or twice I actually entered children's races and won a prizes but it left me with feelings of guilt for not being Greek and not being really invited to the picnic. These Greek people were always friendly and enjoyed their ethnic food and customs.

Picnics happened in Bolus's time and he probably started this but they continued for many years into the mid sixties with the Kowals. One day a Greek boy from my own grade five class in a Toronto public school arrived at one of the picnics. Was he surprised to see me there!

Another way Joe tried to increase the family business was to invite trailers into the park. This led to a full-fledged trailer park on the site. A washroom building and laundry with showers was provided. My grandfather was asked to build wooden boards to house the electric panels for the washroom/shower building and the outdoor lights. I became friends with a number of the trailer park children who lived there year round. Soon, however, the Town of Burlington and Nelson Township authorities were concerned about the presence of trailers in the community. Some people were complaining about the conditions for sanitary living and the environment. Therefore, they tried to get the trailer residents out and close down this part of the Kowal's business. This was the topic of debate at the Nelson Township Council meetings on many occasions. I can see why Joe always seemed worried at the time. Besides, a second trailer park had started up further west off Appleby Line along a creek bed that flowed in to Lake Ontario. Access was obtained through what is now Bryant Crescent off Appleby. I seem to recall mention of this over weeks and months in the local newspapers at the time. In the minutes of the Nelson Township Council in whose jurisdiction this area of what is now Burlington, one can find references to the trailer parks. Knapman's Camp was the second trailer park in the area.

A view of some trailers parked in Lakeshore Trailer Park, circa 1951. Washrooms, showers, and laundry at far right.

DAVID WOODWARD

Apperently the issue for the township Council was that while the trailer population consisted of about 300 people including 100 children, year round residency meant that the children attended local schools but no one was paying taxes to the school board for their education. There was no mechanism for taxing trailer residents at the time. Some councillors wanted to legislate a special tax on Joe Kowal to provide for this but it never came to pass. Joe was also trying to tear down the cabins and build a motel-restaurant around the early fifties and it was an issue for the Township Council also. A neighbour named Wright frequently attended council meetings and complained about zoning and agitated on behalf of some neighbours to get the trailers out. This eventually succeeded, having been the result of health issues for the trailer population over the lack of adequate sewer facilities. The other cause was the lack of taxes being paid by anyone for the trailer park children. There were no sewers or even water pipes along Lakeshore Road at that location then. We had septic tanks with well water pumped into the house and the taps at our house as did all other residents on the lake there. A big part of the business income was lost when the last trailer moved out.

Further out by a huge willow tree about 100 yards from the lake, a local celebrity encamped her trailer for several weeks. She was accompanied by at least one grandchild. Around her trailer she erected a small white picket fence. Her name was Jane Grey and she had a radio talk show on CHML, Hamilton. This lady was really interested in numerology and she once worked at Eatons, in downtown Toronto as a sales clerk. Other celebrities from the wrestling world used to spend summer afternoons in the park and lived at the motel also. One, I remember was called Tex Mackenzie from Texas, of course. He used to polish his decorative leather boots sitting by the edge of the cliff on hot summer days as he prepared for his wrestling match at Maple Leaf Gardens. The boots were yellow and green. Together, we talked about wrestling since my grandmother's nephew, Kenneth Tasker, was a wrestler also. His professional moniker was Tiger Tasker and was often on the bill with Whipper Billy Watson of East York, Toronto.

Lakeshore Park Motel located across from the corner of
Hampton Heath. Photo courtesy of the Kowal Family.

As time went on in the early seventies, Bertha was left
responsible for the park and the motel, it was time to retire.
Joe had passed on. She and her new husband put the park up
for sale and tried to negotiate with the City of Burlington for
a reasonable purchase price. Lakeshore Park had been a park
for as long as anyone could remember and now there was a
possibility that this magnificent promontory on Lake Ontario
would be lost to the community if the city didn't purchase it.
Burlington Council didn't buy it or make a reasonable offer.
Therefore, in 1973 a developer bought it for $244,000 to be
developed into a townhouse site. For me, this was unjust.
I loved that park, having grown up there all my childhood
summers, holidays, and weekends. This was my playground
and it was spacious with lots of grass and trees. I didn't want
it to go private. Many in the community were more than a
bit upset.

Nothing developed on this property for several years. Why?
I do not know but it might have been due to a committee of citizens in Burlington who were concerned with losing access to
the lakeshore waterfront through development. Mary Munro
was one of these, if not the leader. She was elected mayor after
her leadership in the Save the Lakeshore's Association. Joan
Little joined the Burlington Council when she was elected
as a councillor in 1973. It was a time for women to enter
Burlington politics. For my grandparents and myself, the Save
the Lakeshore Association's goals resulted in our being under
threat of losing our private lakefront homes.

In 1974 the City of Burlington purchased the seven acres

DAVID WOODWARD

after all. The price paid to the developer was $1,200,000. I thought of Bertha Kowal who a few short years before received only one-fifth of that amount, she, who put her whole life's work into it. The developers, as always seem to triumph every time. But Bertha had had enough so she didn't hang on. I never heard her express regrets.

By now the John Kolassa farm of 86 acres on the north side of Lakeshore Road had already been developed into Elizabeth Gardens. (1956-58). A drainage pipe into the lake and pumping station were installed there also and a small but busy plaza began to dominate the area. During the years following 1958, the look of the lakeshore in the area changed from a country setting to a suburban environment. It has never been the same since. Zoning on the north side was changed to multi-dwellings from single family residences and town houses sprang up on both sides of Kolassa's former farm house.

Soon enough, the lake started showing stress from the resulting pollution of so many homes emptying their wastewater with soap and chemicals into the new pipes that fed the sewer drain pipes. Algae globs that floated from the bottom to the surface of the lake reached about 100 yards out from the shore. When the water became rough, these strands of yellow-green algae would break off and wash up on the beach rocks. Within a few days the drying and rotting algae began to reek with an offensive odour. Gone were the halcyon days of my childhood when I could swim every day in clean and clear water throughout the summer. Skipping flat stones across the surface of a flat lake was a frequent pastime of every kid in the area. We could still do that and I was 15 or 16 years old. One summer, as they lay a new pipe off the Skyway water plant we watched the night watchman put a lantern on the barge just anchored offshore. It was involved in extending the drainage pipe. He met the local kids by the shoreline as he stood guard over the barge each night and shared many stories of his experiences.

In the late fifties guests of the motel sauntered out for a glimpse of the rising moon. In 1958, we trained the binoculars on the sky above for glimpse of a new age satellite or a NASA balloon. And we actually saw these. On a rare occasion, even northern lights appeared and made us marvel. This was our special world. I still loved going to the park of an evening to strike a conversation with visitors.

Opposite the motel and extending west about 500 yards a developer built what was called Skyway Plaza mentioned above. This is now known as Lakeside Village Shopping Centre and it has known better times. It is badly in need of a makeover but it has been for sale online for some time, said to be owned by an American. It will probably be demolished for homes or multiple dwelling housing if no one will renovate it. In 1958, Skyway Plaza depended on the residents of Elizabeth Gardens and the south east portion of Burlington relied on the plaza for many supplies and services. There was no Burlington Mall or Mapleview Mall then. This was Burlington's first shopping plaza.

The view west along Lakeshore Road. The trailer park is visible at the left.
Today the Lakeside Village Plaza is far right where the house stands.

In that plaza were many wonderful stores to shop in. A grocery store, I think it was a Dominion store, was located where Food Basics is today. Beside that was a Bank of Nova Scotia and next to it a bake shop called Art's Bakery. He was a Dutch man. His wife and he baked the most wonderful cakes, pies, and breads. They lived in the area and served the residents faithfully for many years until Art died. His wife and two children moved to a small farm in Ancaster area. They continued to bake and sell their wares until the early 2000's at the Burlington Mall outdoor market. When my grandparents celebrated their fiftieth anniversary, I ordered a cake for the event from Art's Bakery. During the celebrations, my grandfather bit into his piece of cake and found a gold wedding ring in his mouth. It was Art, the Baker's. He had lost it kneading the flour dough. I was reminded of this by Art's wife many years later as I bought a custard pie at the Burlington Mall market from her. I think she had moved to Ancaster with her two children who were then adults.

Other sites included a department store from Hamilton called Eames. There was a small movie theatre and bowling alley. Still later a Gold's Gym in the corner of the L-shaped plaza was installed. A barber shop and convenience store as well as a drug store and gift shop also existed there. Swiss Chalet came much later as did a bar-restaurant.

Before Art came, we used to have a baker delivery several days a week from Hamilton's Jackson's Bread Company. The truck would arrive and the driver brought his wicker basket of cakes, pies, tarts, and bread to the door- a walk of about 100 feet. He had lost a hand and wrist in WWII and he now carried his basket with a hook. He was always jovial. We also used to have a milkman come five days a week. It was Lakeside Dairy from Brant Street in Burlington. My grandfather built a box which he fastened to the fence for the milk delivery and in which he deposited the money for it. That's how people lived in those days. Service to your door! We also had a milk box built into all the houses in Toronto for the same thing. Those were good times when people paid low price for basic items and when we bought gas, the attendant filled our gas tank, checked the oil, and washed the windshield. No tips were expected and rarely given.

The lake still had some beauty but it wasn't the same until the nineties when phosphates were reduced and more stringent controls enforced. The environment was becoming an issue. We, who still lived on the shore, still loved living there witnessing the constant changes of sky, clouds, and wave action. Wildlife still came — purple martins declined. They lived in apartment-like houses such as my neighbour had built on high poles. We watched as they dove and skimmed the water for mosquitoes and insects. Gulls and the odd Canada goose wafted by all afternoon. In the evening one could often see the stars but not nearly as clearly as in the 50's when lights were few and far between. Now the lights across the lake on the approach to Niagara formed a solid ribbon of glare. But the harvest moons of late September and October shone as beautiful as ever. Yet, no more could I smell the fragrance of berries in the late spring breezes of early June.

Also, the amalgamation of township areas with Burlington, also in 1958, brought with it urban noise and constant agitation. I am glad my early childhood was free from this hectic life. At least I had my memories of an earlier, simpler time. But oh how I miss the early days! Lakeshore Park was a large part of our existence as children. In those summers we swam and dove into the lake diving for white rocks on the bottom. Later we followed intermittently by sunning ourselves and lying on park benches, shivering totally ignorant of the dangers of the sun's rays.

A Burlington council meeting was held and the proposal to acquire homes and properties from Burloak Drive to the former Lakeshore Park passed. Our few neighbours in this stretch of land called a meeting at the old Cantell home, second property from the east. The only time I was ever in that house occurred then. At this time, Cantell's original property was owned by an absentee landlord couple who resided on a farm up Walker's Line, Julia and George Furdos. The host was the tenant, a Mr. Puhlman as the Furdos couple did not yet move to this home. Our discussion centred on what to do about this threat. I was a young adult by now but instinctively knew that my family would probably never have this property far into the future. We feared expropriation but that never happened. Rather, the City and Regional governments followed the plan and just waited until each property owner sold to the municipality willingly. For me, who inherited my grandparents property from my mother who passed away three months after her mother in 1985, it caused more grief. Burlington City Hall would not grant me a permit to improve or enlarge the building. I was out of luck and heart-broken.

Thus, in 1989, I sold the house and land knowing the house my grandfather had built would be demolished. This small piece of property lay smack in the middle of today's park and it now belonged to Halton Region. Directly opposite over the highway sat the farmhouse of Kolassa, many years a child care centre called Parkview. The only consolation was that no one would ever be allowed to own my family's property and I would always be allowed to visit it as public land. If you recall the first chapter, you will see how much I loved this location. My refuge from the big city of Toronto, my paradise when growing up would always be a memory that no one could erase. This realization eased my pain over time, thankfully. Occasionally I visit the surviving Kowal family or Carol Barrowman or the Bristows and we enjoy reminiscing about the bygone times on the lakeshore.

12

In the Vicinity of Burloak Park

About a mile and a half from the Village of Bronte, close to Trafalgar Line, (now Burloak Drive), a Zionist youth camp was built on the north side of Lakeshore Road. There was a rest home for mothers and babes established by the Jewish community around 1933 in Bronte, Ontario. From this initial landmark, the Jewish founders started the camp in what became the Shell property in the fifties. It was 1945 when the land was purchased. This camp was advertised in the Jewish press as follows:

MIZRACHI CAMP GALIL ON LAKE ONTARIO

Above: An advertisement from "The Canadian
Jewish Review", March 10, 1950

The name Mizrachi is a combination of two Hebrew words, "Merkaz" and "Ruchani" – meaning a spiritual centre. To find this camp one would have to walk past the Pig and Whistle Inn at Lakeshore and Burloak and walk east about 300 meters along the north side. There was a long and beautiful unpaved road there leading north. Lining it were many white pines. These have been taken down for development unfortunately.

While going for a walk one January day, I walked up the tree-lined avenue that led to the camp for the first and only time. I was about 16. It was a cold snowy day but I was on holiday and needed an adventure to get out of the house. At the end of the lane, I came across a kind of magnificent two story stone house. I skirted around this almost mansion and found the ruins of the once active Mizrachi camp. There I found an old swimming pool decaying and cracked which had been abandoned years earlier. Some evidence of the structures were there also but very little to indicate it was used in recent days. I do not know when it was sold. The summer campers who went there sometimes paraded along the highway with a horse and buggy to the lakeshore park near our house. There they had a picnic. An old horse pulled a wagon with large milk cans on board for their lunch. Perhaps about twenty people were in the group. Not much more. Sadly, not many people ever remember this as existing.

This camp was apparently located on the Osler Farm Estate of a Major James Osler. Why part of the Osler farm? That apparently is lost to history but there is a reference to the home and estate on the Oakville/Bronte local history site. When I was young I remember us discussing this man and we thought he was Sir William Osler the famous physician who was a founder of the John Hopkin's Medical Centre in Baltimore, Maryland. Osler was a Canadian, born in Dundas, Ontario and trained at McGill in Montreal. He is world famous known to most practising physicians around the world. However, it was not his or his descendant's farm. I believe, it belonged to James Osler, a different family who served in World War I. The barn was large and green with two stories. It was located where the highway does a slight turn about 900 yards east of the Pig and Whistle Inn. A sloping earth ramp located on the east side dominated the building and it was for may years a real architectural gem of a barn typical of many Ontario farms.

Near that location later would be a small golf course just a few hundred feet north of Lakeshore Road on Burloak Drive. Today large homes grace the land there.

The Samuel Curtis House still stands on the corner of Burloak and Lakeshore in Trafalgar, township, now Oakville. Across the road the Original House does not. It was enclosed or partly exists inside a rather large house diagonally opposite the Pig and Whistle Inn. Next to that is situated the Clark House. You can read about the homes in Dorothy Turcotte's book noted in the endnotes.

Shell House, across the road was used for meetings when the company bought it. Before then the family that lived there was called Gudgeon. As a kid I would many times watch the owner land his seaplane off Gudgeon's Point, the promontory that stretches out where the Shell pier is today. Mr. Gudgeon flew home from his work in Hamilton for lunch it seemed.

The now forgotten park erected by Cities Service and Shell at the foot of Great Lakes Boulevard fronting on the lake beside the refinery pier

An old house still existing near there once belonged to a man named Ritchley whom I only met once as he sat on his verandah and I stopped to talk. Just down the street, on the lake side there was park established in the late fifties. It was called Shell Park. The centre piece was a raised reflecting pool that was built to convince everyone that the water in it was being provided cleaner after filtering than on intake. It was lake water used by the gas plant and then put back into the lake purer than taken out. At least that what they said on the sign by the pool. There is still a beautifully landscaped area of flower gardens on the north side of the Lakeshore Road.

The pier they built was built from round supports floated in at the sides of a ship from Toronto. As each support was put into place, it was filled with cement to keep it from moving. The pier still gets ships to take out liquid petroleum or crude. I am not sure which. In the autumn and spring, a station was set up in a small building to observe the migration of birds there. Some people were upset when this part of Shell Park was sold to a developer and that small shack has been replaced by another belonging to Suncor. It stands at the entrance to the pier. In the sixties, in the autumn and spring, the shack was a centre for bird watching as the migration route took the birds over this land point we used to call Gudgeon's Point.

13

On the North Side of Lakeshore Road Opposite Burloak Park

PETER BIELIKOW THE KEEPER OF THE BEEHIVES

On the original farm property opposite Lakeshore Park entrance, resided a family of immigrants from Byelorussia, or White Russia as it was commonly called then. Peter Bielikow and his wife had three daughters, Mary, the eldest, Nadija, the middle child, and Ella, the youngest. They built a modest brick bungalow on the north side of Lakeshore and lived a quiet life. When I was a teenager, about seventeen, I started visiting the youngest daughter there. Peter, was a beekeeper and did that for a living but there were not too many hives as far as I can recall. In the days of the working farm owned by John Kolassa, Peter kept the hives on the farm to assist in the pollination of crops.

Bielikow house on the left, Rudolph house on the right, as seen from the Koleff's driveway

One day I remember coming upon him gathering honey from waxy slabs as he pulled them free. He held the smoker with it's teapot-like spout diverting the bees while he pulled out the slab of honeycomb. I learned that one never approaches the front of the hive to use the smoker. Instead the beekeeper would approach from the side squeezing a white puff wherever there was a bee or slight opening. Then a puff would go around the top edge before he would pry open the lid. The bees swarmed around but only a few landed on him. Indeed, there were two or three large stings evident on his bare chest. Why one would attempt to retrieve the honey shirtless, I cannot fathom but I never asked why. Peter had very limited English anyway and our interactions were always just a smile and short "Hi", or "Hello". When I was older and got to know the family better Peter had passed away before this time and the four women lived by themselves. Mary and Nadija worked regularly outside the home, Mary, being perhaps was a nurse or care giver, and Nadija, a factory worker. Ella was a student.

One day when I first went to see if Ella was home, her mother, Feodosia, invited me in by saying in her broken English, "David, You come my Gome", (pronouncing a hard "g" for the "h" in "home"). While Feodosia spoke very little English she tried to communicate and taught me a dozen or so Russian words. I actually got a library book to practise some words to try to impress them which they appreciated. In Riverdale Collegiate Institute, my Toronto high school at the time, I was studying Latin, Greek, French, and German. So you can see another foreign language was interesting to me. We talked about what they didn't like about the Soviet system of government. The girls and I also discussed the Russian poet, Gorky and writers Dostoyevski, and Tolstoy. I had read <u>Anna Karenina</u> and most of <u>War and Peace</u>. <u>Dr. Zhivago</u> was a popular book I borrowed from the library over that summer. Little did I know how magnificent a movie it would inspire in later years. The movie brought to life the characters in a more meaningful way than I remember from the book version.

Then, Ella and her sisters would turn on the Television to watch *American Bandstand* with Dick Clark. They loved this show and every time I went there that show seemed to be on. Mrs. Bielikow always offered a cup of raspberry tea which she made herself and it was quite and enjoyable drink with cookies.

Over the course of two or three years at my infrequent visits, I noted that a nephthytis plant was positioned on the floor by the side of an archway separating the living and dining rooms. It grew over that time from about three feet in height to cover the edge of the whole arch and start down the other side. Theirs was a simple life but they laughed a lot and seemed to enjoy the freedom way of life in Canada. Mary moved to Toronto later on and I once picked up her sister Ella for a date taking her to a concert at the University of Toronto at Hart House. That was our only date when I was about twenty. I don't believe I ever saw Ella again. She was married and had two or three children. Her mother and two sisters would run into me and my wife in later years occasionally while shopping. When I became a teacher, I remember being contacted by Mary to ask about the progress of her son in a Burlington school. She was asking for advice. When they sold the house and moved I cannot recall and I have not seen any of them in many years.

14

Other Families Opposite Today's Burloak Waterfront Park

THE NOSEWORTHY, HILL, AND RUDOLPH FAMILIES

In 1947, two sisters and their husbands started to build to the east of the Kolassa farmhouse, right next door. They were Irene and Henry Noseworthy and next to that house was the Harvey and Marie Hill house. Noseworthy erected a ranch style white clapboard house of one level and the Hills a red brick bungalow. Henry was a contractor. I believe they came from Hamilton to move out to the suburbs. These neighbours were very friendly and invited us to a party on one occasion. They gave me a glass of ginger ale and I accidentally tipped it over into the record player. Then rushing to mop up the liquid as "Winter Wonderland" played on. I often wonder whether I ruined the turntable. How embarrassing and klutzy on my part! I still feel badly about my clumsiness after all these years. Marie Hill worked in the financial department of the Burlington Board of Education. Irene Noseworthy, her sister, was a bookkeeper. while Harvey Hill worked in the steel industry.

Our front yard with the Noseworthy and Hill homes in the background. Irene Noseworthy sold the house in 1973.

Bill Hubbard, a nephew of theirs, was a boy of my age who visited the Noseworthies often for weeks at a time in the summer. He lived in Hamilton with his parents. He and his red-haired brother, Dan, as well as his blonde sister, were a common sight for many summers there. We often swam in the lake in the afternoons and talked about nature that seemed all around us. Bill and I often hung out together on the farm trying to not get into mischief. We liked to assist in riding the tractor from the barn to the house about supper time. Bill liked to drive the tractor and I seemed to be always stuck with the milk pail trying to keep out straw and dust as we lurched along the uneven rutted road.

During the month of August it eventually got to harvest time for wheat and oats. John Kolassa, the farmer, hired a combine crew to come and cut the wheat fields. I learned what a stook was - a pile of sheaves leaning together in an upright manner so that they would dry out in the sun. Near the barn after some cutting and baling the crew operated the combine to gather the wheat-yielding kernels from the chaff. The straw blew threw an aluminum conduit into a huge haystack from the combine machine.

The wheat grains poured from another aluminum pipe into a small shack until the bins overflowed. Usually I was sent to use a shovel to keep the grain from pouring over the bins onto the floor. I was up to my chest in grain sometimes.

When the job was done we all drank cool well water from a tin cup. Then all the crew and we boys headed off to have a feast. Across from the farm at the Lakeshore Park Motel and Restaurant about 5 or 6 picnic tables were laid end to end and spread with fantastic tasty fare. There were sausages, hot dogs, hamburgers, roast beef, ham, french fries, potato salad, sauerkraut, pickles, and other salads. Lots of soft drinks and lemonade were consumed. Coffee and tea were also available. It remains one of my fondest memories of farm life. Even though I was a city boy, I got to enjoy a rural experience each summer over several years. These days occasionally leap out at me to rekindle smells and sights that delighted me so long ago.

A niece of the Noseworthies called Elodie Matilda I met one day at their home. She and her engaged young man whose name was Earle Rudolph were building a home next to the Bielikows for their impending marriage. Later they lived there for several years often crossing the field to visit their aunt and uncle, the Noseworthies. Later they moved on, selling the house to a couple called Janna and George Lichtenberg. George was an office clerk but I knew nothing else about them.

ZALINSKAS, HARTLEY, SAULEZ AND DEWAR FAMILIES
At the western edge of the farm territory a family from Lithuania resided called Zalinskas. I never really knew this family. The father was an artist named Zigmund and his wife was Ona. However, I do remember that the three or four children had very light blond hair. This plot of land was earlier a vineyard for the Kolassa farm, and today would be located on the Sunrise Retirement Living property at the corner of Hampton Heath and Lakeshore. I recall the home was a wooden clad bungalow but it was solid like the others mentioned above. This house existed where Kolassa had partitioned it off for sale. I suppose partitioning land gave the Kolassas, father and son, extra income to supplement what their mixed farm produced. Further west abutting the Pig and Whistle Inn, several other plots of land with houses had been sold over time by the Cantells and were never part of the Kolassa farm.

Past the Hill residence another bungalow sat with the Hartley family. I believe he and his wife were English. Walter who was an accountant and his wife Rita occasionally were seen about the property and took some interest in local affairs but did not get too involved with the neighbours. We rarely saw them. Eventually they moved in 1973.

Regarding the Saulez family, next to the east, Bertam was a plant worker. He lived with Jane, his daughter, the wife having died early in her life. Jane worked as a machine operator. Later Jane inherited the house and lives there today with her husband, John Gushul.

The Saulez house, still existing

The Dewar family lived in the last house next to the Pig and Whistle. It still stands today. When I first met them, James was the head of the family. He was a draughtsman at the steel company in Hamilton. His father lived in a small house behind the brick dwelling still there. John Dewar, the elder, told my grandfather he was from Belgium originally. He sold or granted this piece of land to James. His son James and his wife had two children, Bob and Patty. Their mother, Madeline, was French Canadian and worked as a waitress at the famous Brant Inn in downtown Burlington. Theirs was a quiet and hardworking family. Bob eventually moved to the Kingston area.

DAVID WOODWARD

The Dewar house still exists

JACHYMEC FAMILY

Between New Street and the Lakeshore are many homes, most of which were built in 1958 as part of Elizabeth Gardens survey. The Kolassa farm was one property that gave rise to this survey and another was the Jachymec family farm. It still stands today after renovations recently.

The Original Jachymec family home on Burloak Drive
south of New Street, originally a farm of 46 acres.

Further west on the lakeshore on the north side several family farms existed also that were gobbled up by the Skyway Plaza. Susan Kalanda and her husband owned one of these farms. They came from Czechoslovakia and had one son, Johnny. Mrs. Kalanda worked very hard in domestic chores while her husband farmed the land. However, she sowed poppy seeds on her front lawn which she added to the breads and rolls she baked. Her kitchen had a large refrigerator stocked with homemade butter and noodles. I enjoyed a cup of tea and watched as she painstakingly cut the flour based dough into long noodle strips. Her home always smelled like a dairy. Outside they had two cows. On her verandah, hung clotheslines on which hung woven cloth rugs which she had made for throw mats. We had quite a few given to us by her. These she made for scraps of cloth cut from linen, nylon, cotton, whatever she had. I never saw Susan that she wasn't working at something. Even outside she sat at a table selling berries and tomatoes in August.

One spring day we visited her home and she was feeding a young fawn. Apparently it showed up in her backyard out of the woods. It seemed to be starving. She put it in a pen and fed it with milk and plantain leaves until the Ontario Department of Natural Resources showed up. They confiscated the baby deer and warned her not to take in wild animals as it was against the law. I remember Mrs. Kalanda crying for days about that as she got very attached to this beautiful-eyed animal. Her husband I rarely saw and he died early leaving Susan a widow. He was not known to speak much English. Nor was he friendly to visitors, I thought. In remembrance of Susan Kalanda let it be known that she was a wonderful neighbour. She was generous and hospitable soul. Everyone loved her for that.

A few houses west sat the DeWitt farm. I did not know them but once went there to buy eggs from their chicken farm.

15
The Pig and Whistle Inn

Long the most obvious landmark in the area of the Burloak Waterfront Park, the Pig and Whistle Inn was built in 1929 by Hughes Cleaver, a Burlington lawyer, developer and sometime Member of Parliament for Burlington. To read about the architecture, history, ownership and details of evolvement over the years, please visit the site of the Burlington Historical Society. There is nothing I can add that would be able to inform the reader of this heritage building better than that site. The archives also contain some historic postcards showing the complex. However, I attach a photograph of part of the building after a small fire there in the early fifties. This photo was taken by the Kowal family and loaned to me for this book.

The Pig and Whistle Inn about 1951 or 52 after a kitchen fire.

Appendix A
Settlers and Owners of the Land Which is Now Burloak Waterfront Park

These people were the ones who actually lived there for periods of time.

In order, east to west and the year the land was purchased

> 1940 - James and Lois Barrowman
> 1941 - Reginald and Mrs. Cantell
> 1954 - Julie and George Furdos
> 1942 - James W. and Hedwig Eales
> 1942 - Fred and Ellen Critchley and in 1968 Aleda
>   Woodward, daughter joined them
> 1985 - David Woodward
> 1949 - James and Phyllis Luckett
> 1954 - Albert W. Jordan
> 1963 - Hugh, Edith and Margaret Landsborough
> 1951 - Kiro and Beatrice Koleff
> 1940 - Samuel and Mrs. Bolus
> 1948 - Joseph and Bertha Kowal

The land for this property was acquired from the Mississauga indigenous nation in 1806 and became Crown Land. The first grantee was Frank Stafford. Over time numerous owners acquired the land there, leaving their names on many east Burlington streets. In the 1900's the property was acquired by one, Frank Hay.

The above names are of those who actually built homes on the property which is now the park. The extreme western property opposite Hampton Heath was the site of a restaurant and cabins built by George Bolus. Later the Kowal family built a motel on the site with a new restaurant and residence. All other properties were bought in order from the town line at the east end and settled by purchasing the land from the daughter of, Frank Hay. Her married name was Marshall and she lived in Detroit.

Regarding a commemorative plaque, at about the time I sold my land next door to Margaret's property, I was invited with two of my neighbours for input to a number of planning committee and advisory meetings through the Burlington Parks Department. We put together early plans for what the park should look like. Now there is a more thorough and final plan for development of the entire park which the Halton Region and City of Burlington designed and which took into consideration our voices at those early meetings. I had asked in writing that a plaque be placed in the new park commemorating the first settlers on the land of the park. They said they would honour that and believe it will be available on the signage in 2018.

Appendix B

Residents and Later owners of Property in Burloak Waterfront Park

Settlers on the Shore in what is today's Burloak Waterfront Park: Years shown are when land was bought.

1. James and Lois Barrowman: Artist   **1940**
    5486 Lakeshore Road.

2. Reginald John & Edna May Cantell: Industrialist   **1941**
    5478 Lakeshore Road

3. George and Julie Furdos Farmer and their tenants
    (Puhlman) and   **1961**
    James W. And Hedwig Eales: Radio Repairman   **1942**
    5460 Lakeshore Road

4. Frederick and Martha Critchley: retired Great War
    veteran. cabinet maker   **1942**
    5454 Lakeshore Road

5. Charles Charles and Gladys Luckett   **1950**
    5448 Lakeshore Road

    James Theodore Luckett Family: **1954**
    Jordan: Gardener, Acrobat, Actor and Vaudevillian   **1954**
    Hugh, Edith and Margaret Landsborough: Scottish
    cabinet maker   **1963**
    Vacant Lot (100 feet) Hugh, Edith & Margaret

Landsborough   **1963**
>**5448 Lakeshore Road**

6.   Kiro and Beatrice Koleff Real Estate Developer   **1950**
>**5434 Lakeshore Road**

7.   Samuel and Sophia Bolus: Restauranteur   **1932**
>**5420 Lakeshore Road**

8.   Joseph and Bertha Kowal Family: Motel-Restaurant
Owner   **1949**
>**5420 Lakeshore Road**

Sold to Acro Development   **1971**
Burlington Purchased property for park about   **1973**

Settlers and Residences on the north side of the Lakeshore Road opposite the park (20th Century) (Year bought shown)

The Pig and Whistle Inn: Old English Inns Limited   **1929**
John Dewar born in Belgium   **1945**
>**5503 Lakeshore Road**

James Saulez and wife, daughter Jane
>**5499 Lakeshore Road**

Owners and sellers of Land on north side of Lakeshore Road in order from the Pig a& Whistle to Hampton Heath (Year bought shown)

Madeleine Dewar, Steel Worker and Waitress at
the Brant Inn   **1945**
Bertram Saulez and wife   **1949**
Rita Helene Hartley   **1959**
Harvey Samuel and Marie Hill   **1958**
Joseph Henry and Irene Noseworthy   **1947**
Dmytro and John Kolassa: Farmer and son   **1947**
Original 86 acre farm built and owned by father

and son   **1947**

5451 Lakeshore Road

Earle George and Elodie Matilda Rudolph   **1952**

5131 Lakeshore Road

Peter Bieliko:Beekeeper

5421 Lakeshore Road

Zalinskas

5411 Lakeshore Road

Beyond the park area west of Hampton Heath on the lake side

Crowell

Landsborough: Hugh, Edith and Margaret lived here
before moving to 5448 Lakeshore in   **1963**

Tomlinson Parents: John and, Children: Barbara,
Bob, Mary Lou,Victor and Richard Family &
Grandmother in a log cabin by the lake   **1947**

Wood: Len and Winnie from Bronte; Len had a peg leg.

Barton:Agnes and Jack, Owner of Agnes Barton Gifts of
Distinction, Gift shop, on New St. at Guelph Line
Dr. Mann, where the Lakeshore Place Retirement
Home stands

North side of Lakeshore Road but facing onto Burloak Drive

Joseph and Mary Jachymek   **1952**

East side of Burloak Drive on north side of Lakeshore Road

Samuel Curtis

Richley

Mizrachi Camp Galil This was a summer camp for
Toronto youth to spread Zionism, built in **1945** and after.

Former Osler Farm - near the corner of Great
Lakes Boulevard

Lake side of Lakeshore east in
Trafalgar Twp. West to East

Clarke, The Original House as described in Dorothy
Turcotte's book, <u>Places and People on Bronte Creek,</u>
self-published, The Ampersand Press, 1993.

Aylesworth

Gudgeon: Later Shell House used as a meeting venue for
a number of years until it burned down. Now it is the site
of a condominium tower.

West of Hampton Heath on north side of Lakeshore.

The Kalanda Family, The DeWitts Egg Farm, and
the Furdos Family Original Farm, which is now
Newport Village.

CONCLUSION

When I decided to write this book, it was because of the people I knew who lived on the land of the present park. Most of these residents are no longer among us. Many were close friends. These people were almost all immigrants to Canada. In a decade or so these newcomers established homes and worked hard to provide for their families. They prospered and in this small area, all getting along and cooperating with each other to achieve their goals. I cannot remember prejudice as being an issue although everyone knew their neighbours and the mostly European countries from which they originated. Today Canadians pride themselves on being a welcoming and tolerant people. I don't remember it being anything else in this semi-rural area. In Toronto, on the other hand, one was more likely to see discrimination as I saw it my neighbourhood in the capital city. Often ethnic groups would be referred to there by disparaging ethnic nicknames. This didn't happen in the Nelson Township area. In any case, I think it is remarkable that in such a small geographic area, each family left a story of their struggle to better themselves in their new land. They deserve to be remembered.

It was my goal to tell stories of the individuals who chose to build a life in a part of Ontario that ended up within the City of Burlington. When they came and selected a plot on a beautiful lake they had no idea of the transformation that would take place in a few generations. Burlington is usually in the top two or three in the best cities in Canada according to the publication, *Money Sense*. Ours was a very small rural community in the very beginning. The only social gathering place there since 1929 was the Pig and Whistle Inn which gave the area a name called Innville. Soon the farms were partitioning land or selling to families for homes in the area and ultimately a subdivision named Elizabeth Gardens was developed.

As the pressures on municipalities along the shore of Lake Ontario led to the disappearance of any lookouts to one of Ontario's Great Lakes, it was inevitable that some political action needed to take place. Thus a cry to save the lakeshore picked up resonance in Burlington in the early seventies. As mentioned in the story, councillors and a far-seeing woman who later became mayor took up the call and did something about it. They made possible a very long stretch of waterfront available to the public for a grand leisure area and lookout.

I have learned a great deal from the families remaining in the area about their trials and pleasures of residence in this place and I am thankful for having had the joy of living here on beautiful Lake Ontario myself. Many changes to complete the Burloak Waterfront Park still need to be done. In the next year or so, it will be complete as a park different from all others that I have had the experience to know. It will be a compliment to the other areas of Burlington such as Beachway Park, Spencer Smith Park, Sioux Lookout, the park at the bottom of Guelph Line in former Port Nelson, and Paletta Park. There will be access to the water in a different way to experience the lake from rocky beaches. Swallows will still flit from their sand-bank nests on the shale cliffs. Children are going to be able to enjoy a splash pad and creative playground fun. Most of all there are areas for nature to display its beauty in the grasses, wild flowers, trees and shrubs of the shore that always were a presence. As I walk along the paved pathway created so all people can enjoy their time there, I walk through the memories of the people in this book. I love remembering the People of Burloak Waterfront Park.

Thanks to the Regional Municipality of Halton and the City of Burlington Park Department for making this possible. It all started with consultations between the city and existing residents who sold their land for the outcome. A community surrounds it but the people who lived here first are mostly gone. I hope you, the reader, gain a bit of knowledge of the historical context of this area through having read about their lives.

DAVID WOODWARD

ENDNOTES

1. The record of land transactions for all Halton County municipalities dating back to the Crown purchase of indigenous lands can be found in the Land Registry Office 20, Halton, 2800 High Point Dr, 2nd Flr, Milton, ON L9T 6P4.

2. This naval battle acquired the name because it looked like a lake regatta off the western site of Fort York in the autumn of 1813. Ships of Her Majesty's fleet circled around each other and tried to get in position to fire on the attacking American fleet. The wind was up to almost gale ferocity and the Americans tried to keep up to the British who had faster ships. Two of the American ships towed militia troops while they attempted to counter the winds, slowing them down.

3. Ration books contained stamp like perforations which could be redeemed when buying food commodities. If you didn't surrender a coupon when attempting to purchase items, you couldn't get those foods. There were also round blue disc-like tokens which were used like coupons to obtain meat products. My family exchanged these valuable tokens and coupons among themselves and extended family so that they were not wasted.

4. Website on which I discovered the trials of the arson court case which concerned the burned Barrowman paintings,;http://krcmar.ca/sites/default/files/2011-10-15_0.pdf

5. The law firm is still in business in Toronto, Osler, Hoskins and Harcourt, LLP.

6. Williamson, Robert J., The Burlington Races Revisited: A Revised Analysis of an 1813 Naval Battle for Supremacy on Lake Ontario, Canadian Military History, Vol. 8 | Issue 4 Article 2.

7. Malcolmson, Robert, Lords of the Lake: The Naval War on Lake Ontario, 1812-1814, Published March 28th 1999 by US Naval Institute Press.

8. A well-known Canadian of vaudeville fame was E. Pauline Johnson, the daughter of Mohawk Chief George H.M. Johnson. Pauline was born at the family home on the Grand River on the Six Nations Reserve near Brantford in 1861. She died in Vancouver and is honoured by a monument with plaque in Stanley Park. where she is buried. A well-known, published poet, singer, and dancer on the stage throughout Canada and parts of the United States, she also visited and entertained in London, England.

9. Albert Foss Tilley: The Legacy of a Canadian Plastic Surgeon: Ca J Plast Surg 2013 Summer ;21(2):102-6.

10. Founded in London, England in 1918 as a military hospital, Westminster Hospital was used to treat veterans suffering from mental illness after World War I. In 1929, Westminster Hospital received its name and also began to accommodate ex-service people who needed medical and surgical treatment. The hospital expanded during World War II to treat the sick and injured from nearby training camps. After the war, the focus returned to long-term and acute care for veterans with disabilities. In 1977, the hospital and its staff and patients were transferred to the Victoria Hospital Corporation, together with 80 acres of land, now LHSC's new Victoria Hospital site at Commissioners Road and Wellington Road. In 1980, Parkwood Hospital assumed responsibility for the care of veterans. Courtesy of London Public Library Image Gallery, http://images.ourontario.ca/london/2416628/data.

11. Sadly, Ollie Bristow in February, 2017 passed away in her 95th year. She had read and approved this chapter.

12. The Koleff-estate home on Crestwood Court was developed by Kiro Koleff and Eric Bristow into ten housing lots one of which was bought by, Dr. A. E. Thibodeau of Burlington.

13. Chopra, Deepak,The Spontaneous Fulfillment of Desire, Harnessing the Infinite Power of Coincidence, Three Rivers Press, New York, 2003.

14. The map at the front of the book was prepared by the author using details from Map No. 26, City of Burlington, Zoning By-Law 2020, and adding details from his own knowledge of what features predated those onto official map No. 26.

15. The map at the back of the book is a map of the master plan of Burloak Waterfront Park as published by the Municipality Halton Region in 2014. All details of the plan are being implemented in 3 stages ending in 2018. Map - thanks to Stirling Todd, Senior Planner, Halton Region

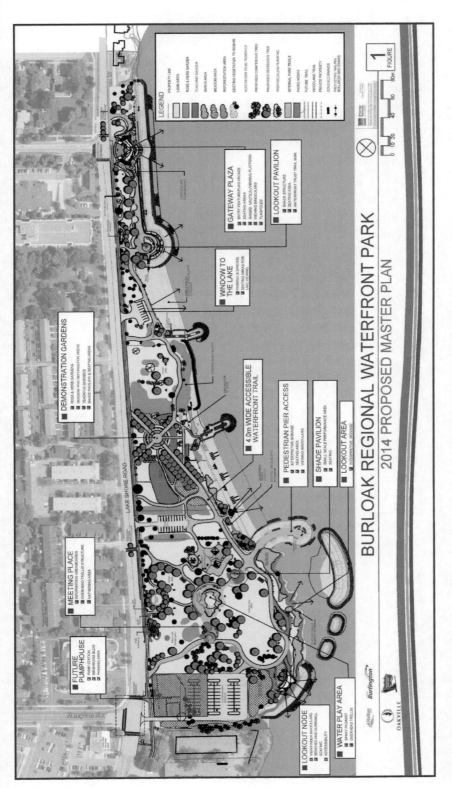

Map of the plan of Burloak Waterfront Park produced by the Region the Municipality Halton in 2014. Reprinted her by permission and courtesy of the same.

Printed in Canada